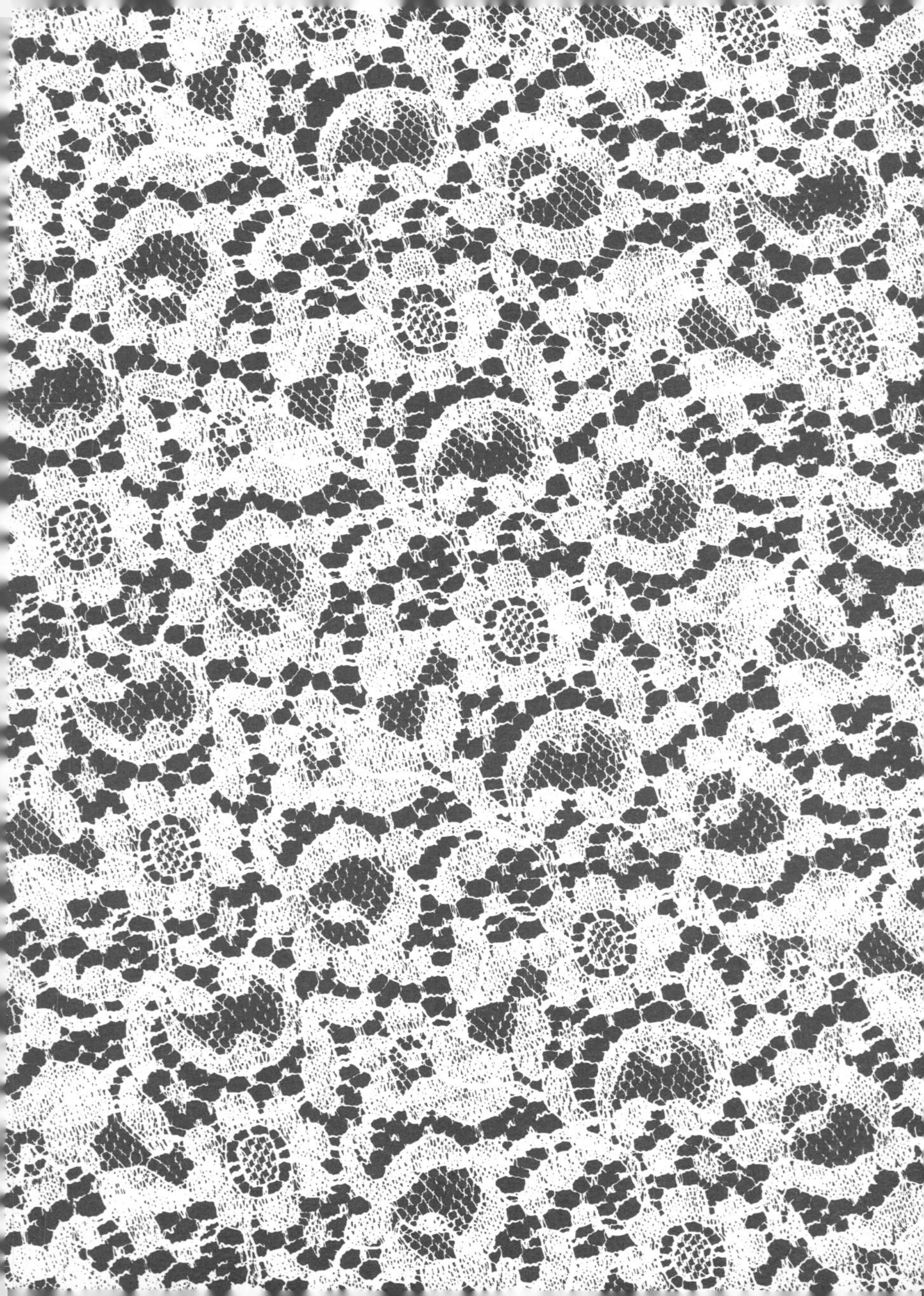

國父遺像

國父遺囑

余致力國民革命凡四十年其目的在求中國之自由平
等積四十年之經驗深知欲達到此目的必須喚起民眾
及聯合世界上以平等待我之民族共同奮鬥
現在革命尚未成功凡我同志務須依照余所著建國方
略建國大綱三民主義及第一次全國代表大會宣言繼
續努力以求貫徹最近主張開國民會議及廢除不平
等條約尤須於最短期間促其實現是所至囑

孫文　三月十一日補簽

中華民國十四年二月二十日

THE THREE PRINCIPLES OF THE PEOPLE

SAN MIN CHU I

By Dr. Sun Yat-sen

Abridged and edited by the Historical Commission of the Kuomintang
Printed and presented by the Publishing Committee for Millions of "SAN MIN CHU I" Copies
Publisher: China Cultural Service
Printer: Yu Tai China Printing Company

CHRONOLOGY OF DR. SUN YAT-SEN

1866 November 12, born in Tsuiheng village, Hsiangshan county, Kwangtung, China.

1879 Went to Hawaii with his mother to join his eldest brother and studied at the Iolani School.

1885 Transferred to Queen's College. Baptized and married. Inspired with thoughts of revolution after China's defeat by France.

1892 Graduated from Hongkong Medical College with honors. Began practice in Macao.

1893 Started revolutionary activities.

1894 Went to Honolulu and founded the Hsing Chung Hui (Revive China Society) after his memorandum to Prime Minister Li Hungchang about national salvation was turned down.

1895 Failed in the first uprising at Canton. Escaped to Hawaii.

1896 Went to London. Kidnaped and detained in the Manchu Legation for two weeds in October before being released upon British intervention arranged by Dr. James Cantlie, his former teacher in Hongkong.

1905 Organized revolutionary groups among Chinese students in Brussels, Berlin and Paris. Founded the Tung Meng Hui (Society of the Common Cause) in Tokyo and was elected president. Proclaimed the Three Principles of the People.

1911 Tenth uprising took the lives of 86 revolutionary martyrs at Canton, March 29. On October 10, the eleventh uprising, started at Wuchang, overthrew Ch'ing Dynasty.

1912 Inaugurated Provisional President of the Republic of China on New Year's Day. Resigned in mid-February to seek peaceful unification of the country. Tung Meng Hui reorganized into the Kuo Min Tang (Nationalist Party), predecessor of later Kuomintang.

1914 Went to Tokyo and reorganized the Kuo Min Tang as the Revolutionary Parry of China.

1915 Directed national movement against Yuan Shih-Kai, his successor in the presidency, who planned to make himself king.

1916 Led revolutionaries in forcing Yuan to abolish the 82-day monarchy.

1917 Established military government in Canton to oppose the warlords of the North.

1919 Reorganized the Revolutionary Party of China as the Kuomintang.

1921 Elected Extraordinary President of the Canton government.

1923 Issued joint statement with Comintern representative Adolf Joffe rejecting Communism for China.

1924 Founded Whampoa Military Academy and appointed Chiang Kai-Shek commandant. Completed lectures on the Three Principles of the People.

1925 Died of cancer in Peiping March 12.

CONTENTS

SAN MIN CHU I

THE PRINCIPLE OF LIVELIHOOD:

DR. SUN YAT-SEN'S WILL

For forty years I have devoted myself to the cause of the people's revolution with but one end in view, the elevation of China to a position of freedom and equality among the nations. My experiences during these forty years have firmly convinced me that to attain this goal we must bring about a thorough awakening of our own people and ally ourselves in a common struggle with those peoples of the world who treat us on the basis of equality.

The work of the Revolution is not yet done. Let all our comrades follow my *Plans for National Reconstruction, Fundamentals of National Reconstruction, Three Principles of the People,* and the *Manifesto* issued by the First National Convention of our Party, and strive on earnestly for their consummation. Above all, our recent declarations in favor of the convocation of a National Convention and the abolition of unequal treaties should be carried into effect with the least possible delay. This is my heartfelt charge to you.

(Signed) SUN WEN
MARCH 11, 1925.

Written on February 20, 1925.

AUTHOR'S PREFACE

After the three volumes of my *Plans for National Reconstruction—Psychological Reconstruction, Material Reconstruction, Social Reconstruction—had been published,** I devoted myself to the writing of *Reconstruction of the State,* in order to complete the series. This book, which was larger than the former three volumes, included *The Principle of Nationalism, The Principle of Democracy, The Principle of Livelihood, The Quintuple—Power Constitution, Local Government, Central Government, Foreign Policy, National Defense,* altogether eight parts. Part One, *The Principle of Nationalism,* had already gone to press; the other two parts on democracy and livelihood were almost completed while the general line of thought and method of approach in the other parts had already been mapped out. I was waiting, for some spare time in which I might take up my

* In 1918.

pen and, without much further research, proceed with the writing. Just as I was contemplating the completion and publication of the book, Ch'en Ch'iung-ming unexpectedly revolted, on June 16, 1922, and turned his guns upon Kwan-yin Shan.** My notes and manuscripts which represented the mental labor of years and hundreds of foreign books which I had collected for reference were all destroyed by fire. It was a distressing loss.

It now happens that Kuomintang is being reorganized and our comrades are beginning to engage in a determined attack upon the minds of our people. They are in great need of the profound truths of *San Min Chu I* and the important in ideas *The Quintuple—Power Constitution* as material for publicity. So I have been delivering one lecture a week. Mr. Hwang Ch'ang-ku is making stenographic reports of the lectures and Mr. Tsou Lu is revising them. The *Principle of Nationalism* series has just been completed and is being published

** A hill in Canton near the headquarters of Dr. Sun.

first in a single volume as a gift to our comrades. In these lectures I do not have the time necessary for careful preparation nor the books necessary for reference. I can only mount the platform and speak extemporaneously, and so am really leaving out much that was in my former manuscripts. Although I am making additions and corrections before sending the book to the press, yet I realize that in clear presentation of the theme in orderly arrangement of the discussion and in the use of supporting facts, these lectures are not at all comparable to the material which I had formerly prepared. I hope that all our comrades will take the book as a basis or as a stimulus, expand and correct it, supply omissions, improve the arrangement and make it a perfect text for publicity purposes. Then the benefits which it will bring to our people and to our state will truly be immeasurable.

SUN WEN

Canton, March 30, 1924

BIOGRAPHICAL SKETCH OF DR. SUN YAT-SEN

Dr. Sun Yat-sen, founder of the Chinese Republic and leader of the Revolution, was born of peasant parentage on November 12, 1866, in a little village near Hsiangshan, a small city in the province of Kwangtung. Here he spent an uneventful childhood attending the village school with the children of the neighborhood. At thirteen years of age he made a trip to Honolulu, where he remained for five years and completed his high school course. There he breathed the spirit of liberty and absorbed freely the influences of American life. When he returned, therefore, to Hongkong and entered Queen's College, he was already dissatisfied with the political life of his own beloved country. Graduating at the age of twenty, he undertook to prepare himself for the medical profession and completed his training in the Hongkong Medical College in the year 1892.

His professional practice, however, was short-lived, for he gave it up to respond to a higher call following China's defeat in the Sino-Japanese War (1894–1895). This was by no means a new enthusiasm but rather a forward step in the career which he had chosen early in his college days. Every day he spent in Hongkong under British rule and every defeat China suffered at the hands of other countries added vigor to his conviction that the government of his own country was rotten to the core. Nothing short of a revolution would provide the remedy. He had dedicated himself to this cause, and among his fellow students he had found a few with whom he could share his deepest aspirations. The task of building up a free and enlightened China became his sole purpose in life.

From the very beginning the undertaking was fraught with dangers. After a hasty attempt at revolt that failed, he embarked in 1895 on his life of exile. Pursued by personal danger he went first to Japan, then to America, and was finally kidnapped on the streets of London and carried off to the Chinese legation, where he was kept hidden for twelve days. Thanks to the loyalty and ingenuity of his friend Dr. James Cantlie he escaped, and the scheme to smuggle him back to China for execution came to naught. He proceeded to Europe and spent the next few years studying the social and political institutions in the countries he visited. During this time he formulated his *Three Principles of the People* and spread his gospel of revolution among his compatriots wherever he went.

After the Boxer trouble in 1900, the cause of the Revolution gained in momentum. The overthrow of the Manchu regime had become a definite program and large numbers of Chinese men and women in all parts of the world joined in the crusade. A conference was held in Tokyo in 1905, at which two important resolutions were passed: (1) that the Revolutionists be united under the name of the Tung

Meng Hui, and (2) that the reigning dynasty be deposed and China transformed into a republic. The membership of the conference included representatives from all the provinces of China and numerous persons from the ranks of Chinese merchants in other lands. The former engaged themselves in an active campaign of secret propaganda in the homeland and the latter opened their purses in unstinted support of these efforts. But for the generous giving of these patriotic businessmen abroad it is improbable that the Revolution could have materialized.

The culmination of these efforts came in the autumn of 1911, when the battle cry was sounded in Wuchang. This capital of Hupeh quickly fell to the Revolutionists. Although the outbreak was precipitated by mistake before the plans were completed, the response in other parts of the country was so widespread that the Revolution was a *fait accompli* in less than one hundred days! The effete Manchu government was overthrown, and Dr. Sun's dream of years had become a reality. His undaunted spirit had won the day and his weary body had earned a momentary rest. He was called upon, however, to become the first president of the new Republic, and hopes ran high that a rejuvenated China would turn a new page in history.

But the events of 1911 proved to be only the beginning of a long process. Broadly speaking two schools of thinking came to dominate the minds of young China, the one led by Yuan Shih-kai and the other by Sun Yat-sen. The former believed in military force, the latter pinned his hope on the awakening of the masses of the poeple. In order that he might better accomplish his purpose, Dr. Sun yielded the presidency to Yuan after he had held it for only three months. He chose to devote himself to the task of educating the people to an understanding of the fundamentals of democracy and of uplifting their economic standards. The Tung Meng Hui was reorganized as a political party with a broader program under the name Kuomintang, and a nation-wide plan of railroad building was undertaken as the first step towards the industrialization of the country. But the personal ambition of Yuan Shih-kai interfered. Instead of giving himself unselfishly to the political reconstruction of the country, he saw in the situation an opportunity for self-aggrandizement. He disregarded Parliament and set out to make himself emperor. Dr. Sun realized too late that his confidence had been misplaced and that the Revolution had been smothered by treason.

This fatal mistake delayed the Revolution until the autumn of 1926, when Chiang Kai-shek finally stepped into the shoes of his deceased leader and led the Nationalist forces on their victorious march from Canton toward the north. Yuan meanwhile had left a legacy of militaristic oppression under which China continues to groan.

But it would be a mistake to think that these sixteen years following the initial success of the Revolution were wasted. Dr. Sun's untiring efforts guided the people of China into a constantly growing patriotism and national consciousness. He attracted to his side many leaders and numberless patriots eager to undertake the task of carrying on the Revolution to a finish. The more he met with reverses the stronger became his hold on his followers. Several times he set up a separate government in Canton and as often his plans were frustrated, until finally in 1923 a stable regime was established and a demonstration of efficient and effective government was made. During this period he reorganized the Kuomintang for the third time and made clear the practice of party government. He elaborated his political philosophy of the Three Principles in a series of popular lectures, and sounded the clarion call with respect to the unequal treaties. These achievements constitute the basic ideals and policies of the Revolutionary movement. The Three Principles inspired the people with a political ideal, and the denunciation of the unequal treaties released a latent force in the hearts of the people nurtured by the inarticulate desires of many years. Dr. Sun Yat-sen was a diligent student, a farsighted statesman, an indefatigable worker, an irrepressible optimist and, above all, he was China's beloved leader, clear of vision and steadfast in purpose. He not only blazed the trail in the reconstruction of new China, but he also laid down the highways leading towards the successful consummation of his ideals in the future. Out of his years of trial and travail he discovered for coming generations a sure way for the recovery of national freedom.

On March 12, 1925, when the unification of China was apparently within reach, he died in Peking. For a short while rumors were rife reporting the disintegration of the party which he had founded and had taken pains to build up. But the fact was quickly revealed that the party was stronger than ever after his death. His indestructible spirit gripped the lives of his followers even more powerfully than before. It is sometimes even suggested that his death has actually served to accelerate the progress of the Revolution.

But in the thinking of Dr. Sun the Revolution is a continuous process. This "period of military achievement" represents only its beginning and is of less importance than the "period of training" which is to follow. Only when the training process is completed can the Revolution bring the country to the full enjoyment of democracy. In his own words uttered on his deathbed, "The Revolution is not yet completed. All my comrades must strive on."

Dr. Sun died a comparatively poor man, leaving behind no property except a house which his adherents overseas had bought for him over ten years ago, and a library said to be one of the best on social and political sciences in existence. For forty years he toiled "in order to achieve freedom and equality for China." He is the father of new China, taking his place among the foremost leaders in history.

Shanghai, 1927. **L. T. CHEN**

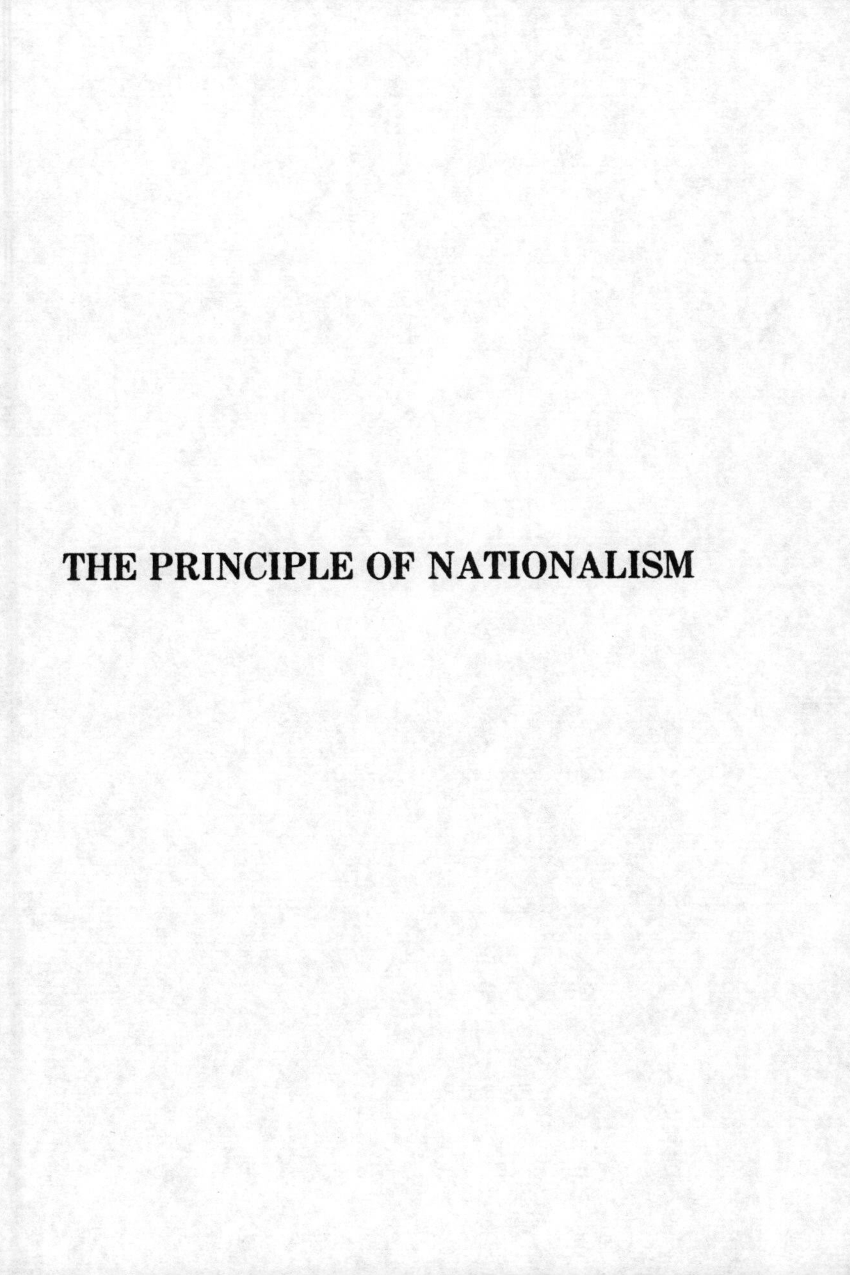

THE PRINCIPLE OF NATIONALISM

LECTURE ONE

Delivered on January 27, 1924.

Gentlemen: I have come here to-day to speak to you about the *San Min* Principles. What are the *San Min* Principles? They are, by the simplest definition, the principles for our nation's salvation. What is a principle? It is an idea, a faith, and a power. When men begin to study into the heart of a problem, an idea generally develops first; as the idea becomes clearer, a faith arises; and out of the faith a power is born. So a principle must begin with an idea, the idea must produce a faith, and the faith in turn must give birth to power, before the principle can be perfectly established. Why do we say that the *San Min* Principles will save our nation? Because they will elevate China to an equal position among the nations, in international affairs, in government, and in economic life, so that she can permanently exist in the world. The *San Min* Principles are the principles for our nation's salvation; is not our China to-day, I ask you, in need of salvation? If so, then let us have faith in the *San Min* Principles and our faith will engender a mighty force that will save China.

What is the Principle of Nationalism? I would say briefly that the Principle of Nationalism is equivalent to the "doctrine of the state." The Chinese people have shown the greatest loyalty to family and clan with the result that in China there have been family-ism and clanism but no real nationalism. Foreign observers say that the Chinese are like a sheet of loose sand. Why? Simply because our people have shown loyalty to family and clan but not to the nation—there has been no nationalism. The family and the clan have been powerful unifying forces; again and again the Chinese have sacrificed themselves, their families, their lives in defense of their clan. But for the nation there has never been an instance of the supreme spirit of sacrifice. The unity of the Chinese people has stopped short at the clan and has not extended to the nation.

My statement that the principle of nationality is equivalent to the doctrine of the state is applicable in China but not in the West. For the reason that China, since the Ch'in and Han dynasties, has been developing a single state out of a single race, while foreign countries have developed many states from one race and have included many nationalities within one state. For example, England, now the world's most powerful state, has, upon the foundation of the white race, added brown, black, and other races to form the British Empire; hence, to say that the race or nation is the state is not true of England. We all know that the original stock of England was the Anglo-Saxon race, but it is not limited to England; the United States, too, has a large portion of such stock. So in regard to other countries we cannot say that the race and the state are identical; there is a definite line between them.

How shall we distinguish clearly between the two? The most suitable method is by a study of the forces which molded each. In simple terms, the race or nationality has developed through natural forces, while the state has developed through force of arms. To use an illustration from China's political history: Chinese say that the *wangtao,* royal way or way of right, followed nature; in other words, natural force was the royal way. The group molded by the royal way is the race, the nationality. Armed force is the *pa-tao,* or the way of might; the group formed by the way of might is the state. Since of old, no state has been built up without force. But the development of a race or nationality is quite different: it grows entirely by nature, in no way subject to force. Therefore, we say that a group united and developed in the royal way, by forces of nature, is a race; a group united and developed by the way of might, by human forces, is a state. This, then, is the difference between a race or nationality and a state.

Again, as to the origin of races. Man was originally a species of animal, he is far removed from the common fowl and the beasts; he is "the soul of all creation." Mankind is divided first into the five main races—white, black, red, yellow, brown. Dividing further, we have many subraces, as the Asiatic races—Mongolian, Malay, Japanese, Manchurian, and Chinese. The forces which developed these races were, in general, natural forces, but when we try to analyze them we find they are very complex. The greatest force is common blood. Chinese belong to the yellow race because they come from the blood stock of the yellow race. The blood of ancestors is transmitted by heredity down through the race, making blood kinship a powerful force.

The second great force is livelihood; when the means used to obtain a living vary, the races developed show differences. The Mongolians' abode, for instance, folllowed water and grass; they lived the life of nomads, roaming and tenting by water and grass, and out of these common nomadic habits there developed a race, which accounts for the sudden rise of Mongol power.

The third great force in forming races is language. If foreign races learn our language, they are more easily assimilated by us and in time become absorbed into our race. On the other hand, if we know the language of foreign countries, we are in trun easily assimilated by foreigners. If two peoples have both common blood and common language, then assimilation is still easier. So language is also one of the great forces for the development of a race.

The fourth force is religion. People who worship the same gods or the same ancestors tend to form one race. Religion is also a very powerful factor in the development of races.

The fifth force is customs and habits. If people have markedly similar customs and habits, they will, in time, cohere and form one race. When, therefore, we discover dissimilar peoples or stocks amalgamating and forming a homogeneous race, we must attribute the development to these five forces—blood kinship, common language, common livelihood, common religion, and common customs—which are products not of military occupation but of natural evolution. The comparison between these five natural forces and armed force helps us to distinguish between the race or nationality and the state.

Considering the law of survival of ancient and modern races, if we want to save China and to preserve the Chinese race, we must certainly promote Nationalism. To make this principle luminous for China's salvation, we must first understand it clearly. The Chinese race totals four hundred million people; for the most part, the Chinese people are of the Han or Chinese race with common blood, common language, common religion, and common customs—a single, pure race.

What is the standing of our nation in the world? In comparison with other nations we have the greatest population and the oldest culture, of four thousand years' duration. We ought to be advancing in line with the nations of Europe and America. But the Chinese people have only family and clan groups; there is no national spirit. Consequently, in spite of four hundred million people gathered together in one China, we are in fact but a sheet of loose sand. We are the poorest and weakest state in the world, occupying the lowest position in international affairs; the rest of mankind is the carving knife and the serving dish, while we are the fish and the meat. Our position now is extremely perilous; if we do not earnestly promote nationalism and weld together our four hundred millions into a strong nation, we face a tragedy the loss of our country and the destruction of our race. To ward off this danger, we must espouse Nationalism and employ the national spirit to save the country.

Now compare the rate of increase of the world's populations during the last century: the United States, 1,000 per cent; England, 300 per cent; Japan, also 300 per cent; Russia, 400 per cent; Germany, 250 per cent; France, 25 per cent. The large gain has been due to the advance of science, the progress of medicine, and yearly improvement of hygienic conditions, all of which tend to reduce the death rate and augment the brith rate. What is the significance for China of this rapid growth of other populations? When I compare their increase with China's, I tremble.

Within the next century the world's population will surely multiply several times. When we compare the total surface of the earth with the number of inhabitants, we see that the world is already suffering from overpopulation. The recent European War, some have said, was a fight for a "place in the sun." The European powers, to a large extent, are near the frigid zone, so one of the causes of the war was the struggle for equatorial and temperate land, a struggle indeed for more sunlight. China has the mildest climate and the most abundant natural products of any country in the world. The reason why other nations cannot for the present seize China right away is simply because their population is yet smaller than China's. A hundred years hence, if their population increases and ours does not, the more will subjugate the less and China will inevitably be swallowed up. Then China will not only lose her sovereignty, but she will perish, the Chinese people will be assimilated, and the race will disappear. The Mongol and the Manchu conquerors of China used a smaller number to overcome a larger and tried to make the larger number their slaves. If the Powers some day subjugate China, it will be large numbers overcoming a smaller number. And when that time comes, they will have no need of us; then we will not even be qualified to be slaves.

LECTURE TWO

Delivered on February 3, 1924.

From ancient times, the increase and the decrease of population has played a large part in the rise and fall of nations. This is the law of natural selection. Since mankind has not been able to resist the forces of natural selection, many ancient and famous nations have disappeared without leaving a trace. Our Chinese nation is one also of great antiquity, with more than four thousand years of authentic history. Although from time immemorial we have been profoundly affected by natural forces, yet Nature has not only perpetuated the race but has made us extremely prolific. We have grown to four hundred millions and are still the world's most numerous and largest nation; we have enjoyed the blessings of Nature in greater measure than any other nation, so that through four millenniums of natural experiences, human movements, and varied changes we see our civilization only advancing and our nation free from decay. One generation has succeeded another and we are still the world's most cultured people. Hence a certain class of optimists, just because the Chinese nation has survived innumerable disasters in the past, hold that the nation cannot perish in the future, come what may. This sort of talk and hope, I think, is wrong. If it were a matter merely of natural selection, our nation might survive, but evolution on this earth depends not alone on natural forces, it depends on a combination of natural and human forces. Human agencies may displace natural agencies and "the work of man overcome Heaven." Of these man-made forces the most potent are political forces and economic forces. They have a greater influence upon the rise and fall of nations than the forces of Nature, and our nation, caught in the current of modern world movements, is not only feeling the pressure of these two forces but is being overwhelmed in the evils that result from them.

China in these thousands of years has been twice crushed by political power to the point of complete subjection, during the Mongol and Manchu dynasties. But both these times we lost our country to a smaller not a larger people. Hence, although China has been twice subjected politically, the race has not been seriously injured.

But political and economic forces work more rapidly than the forces of natural selection and can more easily extirpate a great race. China, if she were affected only by natural selection, might hold together another century; but if she is to be crushed by political and economic power, she will be annihilated by the peoples of the Great Powers. And should the whole number not perish this way, there are still the natural forces to wipe us out. From now on the Chinese people will be feeling the pressure simultaneously of natural, political, and economic forces. So you see what a critical time it is for our race!

China has been under the political, domination of the West for a century. During the past century China has lost a huge amount of territory. The Powers' attitude was formerly something like this: since China would never awaken and could not govern herself, they would occupy the points along the coast like Dairen, Weihaiwei, and Kowloon as bases for "slicing up" China. Then when the Revolution broke out in China, the Powers realized that China still had life, and therefore gave up the idea for partitioning her. When the Powers had their greedy eyes on China, some counter-revolutionists said that Revolution would only invite dismemberment; but the result was just the opposite, for it frustrated foreign designs upon China.

Further back in history, our territorial losses were Korea, Taiwan (Formosa), the Pescadores, and such places, which as a result of the Sino-Japanese War, were ceded to

Japan. Still further back in the century, we lost Burma and Annam. China did put up a slight opposition at the time to giving up Annam. China did put up a slight opposition at the time to giving up Annam. In the battle of Chen-Nan-Kuan (Southern Frontier) China was really victorious but was so overawed later by France that she made peace and was compelled to cede Annam to France. Annam and Burma were both formerly Chinese territory; as soon as Annam was ceded to France, England occupied Burma. Still earlier in the history of territorial losses were the Amur and Ussuri river basins and before that areas north of the Ili, Khohand, and Amur rivers—the territory of the recent Far Eastern Republic—all of which China gave over with folded hands to the foreigner without so much as a question. In addition there are those small countries which at one time or another paid tribute to China—the Loochoo Islands, Siam, Borneo, the Sulu Archipelago, Java, Ceylon, Nepal, Bhutan.

In its age of greatest power, the territory

of the Chinese Empire was very large, extending northward to the north of the Amur, southward to the south of the Himalayas, eastward to the China Sea, westward to the T'sung Lin.

After the Chinese Revolution, the Powers realized that it would be exceedingly difficult to dismember China by political force. A China which had learned how to revolt against the control of the Manchus would be sure some day to oppose the political control of the Powers. As this would put them in a difficult position, they are now reducing their political activities against China and are using economic pressure instead to keep us down. Economic oppression is more severe than political oppression. Political oppression is an apparent thing. The common people are easily provoked by political oppression but are hardly conscious of economic oppression. China has already endured several tens of years of economic domination from the Powers and nobody has felt irritated at all.

The result is that China is everywhere becoming a colony of the Powers. The people of the nation still think we are only a "semi-colony" and comfort themselves with this term, but in reality we are being crushed by the economic strength of the Powers to a greater degree than if we were a full colony. China is not the colony of one nation but of all, and we are not the slaves of one country but of all. I think we ought to be called a "hypo-colony."

Now how do other countries meet foreign economic pressure and check the invasion of economic forces from abroad?—Usually by means of a tariff which protects economic development within these countries. Just as forts are built at the entrances of harbors for protection against foreign military invasion, so a tariff against foreign goods protects a nation's revenue and gives native industries a chance to develop. The idea of a protective tariff is to put a heavy duty on imports. The high duty makes foreign goods expensive so that they cannot circulate, while native goods free from duty are reasonably priced and widely distributed.

What is the situation now in China? Before China had a foreign trade, the goods used by the people were handmanufactured by themselves. The ancient saying "man tills and woman weaves" shows that agriculture and cloth making are old industries in China. Then foreign goods began to come in. Because of the low tariff, foreign cloth is cheaper than native cloth. Since, moreover, certain classes of the people prefer the foreign to the native cloth, native industry has been ruined. With the destruction of this native hand industry, many people have been thrown out of work and have become idlers. This is a result of foreign economic oppression. So, political oppression can be easily seen even by the ignorant classes, but economic oppression is an intangible thing which none of us can easily perceive. One can even load heavy burdens on oneself. Since China opened foreign trade, the unfavorable balance of trade is steadily becoming rampant.

Then there is the economic domination of foreign banks. The Chinese psychology now is one of distrust toward the native banks and of extreme confidence in the foreign banks. Some people are even willing to store up foreign paper currency in perference to Chineses silver currency. And the reason is that the common people have been poisoned by the influence of foreign economic domination.

Besides the foreign bank notes, there is bank exchange. We Chinese in the ports trust the foreign banks also in the exchange of our money. But, in making exchange for the Chinese, the foreign bank charges not only the customary bank rate of one half per cent but seizes profits in other ways.

The power of the foreign banks in China is seen also in their bank deposits. If a Chinese has money and wants to deposit it in a bank, he does not wait to ask whether the Chinese bank has a large or small capital or gives high or low interest. As soon as he knows that the bank is managed by his own country men, he immediately feels that it is probably not safe and that it would not do to risk his deposits there. He does not ask whether the foreign bank is reliable or not, whether it pays high or low interest; if he hears that the bank is run by foreigners and hangs out a foreign sign, he swallows the sedative, feels very safe and invests his money. Even if the interest is very low, he is quite satisfied. Thus the foreign banks, with no trouble except that of handling the money, take Chinese capital and earn interest from it. The reason for all this loss of interest to foreigners is again the vitiating influence of foreign economic control. The total profits of the foreign banks alone, in paper money issues, in exchange and deposit banking, must be around $100,000,000 a year.

Besides the foreign banks, there are freight rates. Chinese goods sent abroad have to depend on foreign bottoms, and even goods sent to interior points, as Hankow, Changsha, and Canton, are carried largely by foreign ships. If

China exports $100,000,000 worth of goods to Europe, she must pay $10,000,000 for freight.

There is yet one more loss to consider—that from the speculation business. Foreigners in the concessions take advantage of a weak point—avarice—in the Chinese character and provide daily opportunities for small speculation, and every few years some big opportunity which arouses the gambling passion of the Chinese to fever heat. And the ordinary small speculative businesses amount, in the end, to high figures.

Because of this economic mastery of China and the consequent yearly damages, our society is not free to develop and the common people do not have the means of living. This economic control alone is worse than millions of soldiers ready to kill us. And while foreign imperialism backs up this economic subjugation, the living problems of the Chinese people are daily more pressing, the unemployed are daily increasing, and the country's power is, in consequence, steadily weakening.

Within the last hundred years, China has begun to suffer from the population problem: the Chinese people are not increasing, while other populations are growing. Now we are suffering also from political and economic domination. If we can no longer find a solution for these three pressing problems, then, no matter how large China's area or how great her population, another century will see our country gone and our race destroyed. Now that we realize the seriousness of political domination and the even greater seriousness of economic domination, we cannot boast that China's four hundred millions will not be easily exterminated. Never before in all her millenniums of history has China felt the weight of three such forces at one and the same time. For the future of the Chinese nation we must find a way to break them!

LECTURE THREE

Delivered on February 10, 1924.

Nationalism is that precious possession which enables a state to aspire to progress and a nation to perpetuate its existence. China to-day has lost that precious possession. Why? To answer that question and to study whether we have really lost our national spirit is my theme to-day.

To me it is clear that we have lost it not for a day but for centuries. Just look at the anti-revolution articles which came out before the Revolution, all opposing nationalism! For hundreds of years the idea of nationalism had been dead in China; in all the literature of this time one can hardly catch any note of nationalism.

To-day I want to talk to you about some of the reasons for this loss of our nationalism. There are many reasons, of which the greatest is our subjection to alien races. When one race conquers another, it naturally does not allow the subject people to have independent thought. Japan, for example, now that it has control of Korea, is trying to convert the minds of the Koreans. All nation alistic ideas are expunged from Korean school texts, so that thirty years from now Korean children will not know there is a Korea or that they are Koreans. The conquering people tries to destroy that precious possession of the subject people.

China's nationalism was originally crushed out by alien rule, yet there have been other subjugated races than the Chinese. The Jews lost their country and before Jesus' day had become a conquered people. When Jesus was preaching, his followers took him for a revolutionist and wanted him to become a revolutionary leader; he was called the "King of the Jews." It is probable that Jesus' religion did contain some ideas of political revolution, yet one of his disciples thought the political revolution had failed and betrayed his teacher. He did not comprehend that Jesus was a religious revolutionist who called his country the Kingdom of Heaven. So, although their state was destroyed, the Jewish race itself has survived since the time of Christ. Or consider Poland, which, although it was a subject nation for a hundred years, has an unquenchable national consciousness; so after the European War the Poles revived their old state. Thus compared, China is seen to be a subject nation similar to Judea and Poland; then, why have they not lost their national spirit while China, after two periods of subjugation, has had all her national pride crushed out? It is a very strange fact and the study of its causes is very interesting. Before China was subjugated, she had a very cultured people and a powerful state. She called herself the "majestic nation," the "land of famous letters and objects," and looked on other countries as barbarian; she thought she was situated in the center of the world and so named herself the "Middle Kingdom." Other expressions, as the "Great Unifier," "Heaven has but one sun, people have but one King," "Gentry of all nations bow before the crown and pearls," date from before the period of China's subjection, when her nationalism was slowly evolving into cosmopolitanism. If we follow out this line of thought, we will begin to see why China has lost her national spirit while other races, as the Jews, have kept theirs for two thousand years, and why China has been a subject nation for only three hundred years, yet all her nationalism has vanished.

To study the cause is like diagnosing a sick man. Whatever disease a man contracts can be traced back either to a poor constitution or to some weakness before he was taken sick. Before China lost her sovereignty, there were already roots of disease in her system which, as soon as she suffered conquest, caused her national mind to decay.

A new theory is emerging in England and

Russia, proposed by the intellectuals, which opposes nationalism on the ground that it is narrow and illiberal—simply a doctrine of cosmopolitanism. England now, and formerly Russia and Germany, together with modern young advocates of new culture in China, support this doctrine and decry nationalism. I constantly hear young men saying, "The *San Min* Principles are not adapted to the tendencies of modern time; the latest and best doctrine is that of cosmopolitanism." Is it really? Then why did China, as soon as she was conquered, lose all her national spirit? Cosmopolitanism is the same thing as China's theory of world empire two thousand years ago. When we study this theory, do we find it good or not? We cannot decide whether an idea is good or not without seeing it in practice. If the idea is of practical value to us and to the world, it is good, if the idea is impractical, it is no good.

The nations which are employing imperialism to conquer others and which are trying to maintain their own favored positions as sovereign lords of the whole world are advocating cosmopolitanism and want the world to join them.

There are several great states, the so-called Great Powers, whose policies and character have not yet undergone any marked change. But in the future, England and the United States may be able to break up the group of powers and become the only great powers. Suppose that should happen and then that England should subjugate China and our people become English-would that be good for us? If Chinese should become naturalized British or Americans and help England or America to destroy China, saying that we were but following out the principle of cosmopolitanism, would our consciences, let me ask you, be at rest? If our consciences hurt us at all, it would be because we had some nationalistic feelings; so, I say, nationalism is that precious possession by which humanity maintains its existence. If nationalism decays, then when cosmopolitanism flourishes we will be unable to survive and will be eliminated by other races. Have we a strong or a weak race, a fit or an unfit race? Not one of us is willing to see our race perish or fail; everyone wishes the race to survive and to win out these are natural, instinctive feeings. But our country to-day is in a very perilous position. Because we have lost our national spirit, we have opened the gates for political and economic forces to break in, which never would have happened if we had preserved our nationalism.

It is difficult to explain just how we have lost our nationalism. To illustrate I will tell a story which may seem off the point and unrelated to our thesis, but perhaps it will make clearer the causes of which we are speaking. It is an incident which I personally witnessed in Hongkong. There was a coolie who worked daily at the steamer jetties carrying passengers' baggage with his bamboo pole and two ropes. Each day's load was his means of livelihood for that day, but he finally managed to save more than ten dollars. The Luzon lotteries were flourishing at that time and this coolie used his savings to buy a Luzon lottery ticket. He had no home and no place to keep his things or the lottery ticket which he had bought. All his tool of trade was his bamboo pole and two ropes which he carried about with him everywhere he went. So he hid the lottery ticket inside of his bamboo pole, and since he could not always be pulling out the ticket to be looking at it, he fixed the number indelibly on his mind and thought about it all the time. When the day for the drawing came, he went to the lottery shop to match this number, and as soon as he saw the list of numbers he knew that he won first prize, acquiring a wealth of $100,000. He was in ecstasy, almost insane with joy. Thinking that he would no longer have to be a coolie and use his bamboo pole and ropes, that he would be a rich man forever, he gleefully took the pole and ropes and threw them into the sea!

The coolie's bamboo pole may represent

nationalism—a means of existence; the winning of the first prize may represent the time when China at the zenith of her power was evolving into cosmopolitanism and when our forefathers, believing that China was the world's great state—that "Heaven has but one sun, people but one king"; that "gentry of all nations bow before the crown and pearls"; that universal peace would henceforth prevail and that the only thing necessary was a world harmony in which the world would bring its tribute to China—threw away nationalism as the coolie threw his bamboo pole into the sea. Then when China was overcome by the Manchus, she not only failed to become the master of the world, but even failed to keep her small family property intact. The national spirit of the people was destroyed, just as the bamboo pole was thrown into the sea.

Those young students who prate about the new culture and espouse cosmopolitanism, saying that nationalism is out of date, might have some ground if they spoke for England

and America or even our forefathers, but if they think they are speaking for the Chinese today, we have no place for them. If our forefathers had not thrown away the bamboo pole, we might have won first prize, but we threw away the pole too early, forgetting that the ticket was hidden inside. As soon as we felt the yoke of foreign political and economic domination and encountered the forces of natural selection, we came face to face with the tragic possibility of a lost nation and a vanishing race.

If we Chinese can in the future find some way to revive our nationalism, can discover another bamboo pole, then no matter what foreign political and economic forces oppress us, we will survive through the ages. We can overcome the forces of natural selection; Heaven's preservation of our four hundred millions of Chinese till now shows that it has not wanted to destroy us; if China perishes, the guilt will be on our own heads and we shall be the world's great sinners. Heaven has placed great responsibilities upon us Chinese; if we do not love ourselves, we are rebels against Heaven. China has come to the time when each one of us has a great responsibility to shoulder. If Heaven does not want to eliminate us, it evidently wants to further the world's progress. If China perishes, she will perish at the hands of the Great Powers; those Powers will thus be obstructing the world's progress. If we want to resist Might we must espouse nationalism and in the first instance attain our own unity, then we can consider others and help the weaker, smaller peoples to unite in a common struggle against the oppressors. Together we shall use Right to fight Might, and when Might is overthrown and the selfishly ambitious have disappeared, then we may talk about cosmospolitanism.

LECTURE FOUR

Delivered on February 17, 1924.

Before the European War all the European nations had been poisoned by imperialism. What is imperialism? It is the policy of aggression upon other countries by means of political force, or, in the Chinese phrase, "long-range aggression." As all the peoplse of Europe were imbued with this policy, wars were continually breaking out; almost every decade had at least one small war and each century one big war. The greatest of all was the recent European War, which may be called the World War because it finally involved the whole world and pulled every nation and people into its vortex. The causes of the European War were, first, the rivalry between the Saxon and Teutonic races for control of the sea. Germany in her rise to greatness had developed her navy until she was the second sea power in the world; Great Britain wanted her own navy to rule the seas so she tried to destroy Germany, whose sea power was next to hers. From this struggle for first place on the sea came the war.

A second cause was each nation's struggle for more territory. In eastern Europe there is a weak state called Turkey. For the past hundred years the people of the world have called it the "sick man of Europe." Because the government was unenlightened and the sultan was despotic, it became extremely helpless and the European nations wanted to partition it. Because the Turkish question had not been solved for a century and every nation of Europe was trying to solve it, war resulted. The first cause of the European War, then, was the struggle between white races for supremacy; the second cause was the effort to solve critical world problems. One side in the war was called the Entente; the other side , the Allied Powers. The Allied

Powers* at first included Germany and Austria; Turkey and Bulgaria later joined them. The Entente Powers** at first were Serbia, France, Russia, England, and Japan; Italy and the United States joined afterwards. The United States' entry into the war was due entirely to racial considerations. During the first two years of the war Germany and Austria were in the ascendancy. Paris and the English Channel were almost captured by the German and Austrian armies. The Teutons thought that Great Britain was certainly done for, and the British themselves were thoroughly alarmed. Seeing that the American people are of the same race as they, the British used the plea of race relationship to stir up the people of the United States. When American realized that England, of her own race, was in danger of being destroyed by Germany, of an alien race, inevitably "the creature sorrowed for its own kind" and America threw in her lot with

* Central Powers.

** "Allies."

England to defend the existence of the Anglo-Saxons. Moreover, fearing that her own strength would be insufficient, America tried with all her might to arouse all the neutral countries of the world to join in the war to defeat Germany.

During the war there was a great phrase, used by President Wilson and warmly received everywhere "self-determination of peoples." Because Germany was striving by military force to crush the peoples of the European Entente, Wilson proposed destroying Germany's power and giving autonomy henceforth to the weaker and smaller peoples. His idea met a world welcome. As a result of the noble theme propounded by the Entente all the oppressed peoples of Europe and of Asia finally joined together to help them in their struggle against the Allied Powers. At the same time, Wilson proposed, to guard the future peace of the world, fourteen points, of which the most important was that each people should have the right of self-determination. When victory and defeat still hung in the balance, England and France heartily indorsed these points, but when victory was won and Peace Conference was opened, England, Frace, and Italy realized that Wilson's proposal of feedom for nations conflicted too seriously with the interests of imperialism; and so, during the conference, they used all kinds of methods to explain away Wilson's principles. The result was a peace treaty with most unjust terms; the weaker, smaller nations not only did not secure self-determination and freedom but found themselves under an oppression more terrible than before. This shows that the strong states and the powerful races have already forcibly take possession of the globe and that the rights and privileges of other states and nations are monopolized by them. Hoping to make themselves forever secure in their exclusive position and to prevent the smaller and weaker peoples from again reviving, they sing praises to cosmopolitanism,saying that nationalism is too narrow; really their espousal of internationalism is but imperialism and aggression in another guise.

But Wilson's proposals, once set forth, could not be recalled; each one of the weaker, smaller nations who had helped the Entente to defeat the Allied Powers and had hope to attain freedom as a fruit of the victory was doomed to bitter disappointment by the results of the Peace Conference. Then Annam, Burma, Java, India, the Malay Archipelago, Turkey, Persia, Afghanistan, Egypt, and the scaves of weak nations in Europe, were stirred with a great, new consciousness; they saw how completely they had been deceived by the Great Powers' advocacy of self-determination and began independently and separately to carry out the principle of the "self-determination of peoples."

Many year of fierce warfare had not been able to destroy imperialism because this war was a conflict of imperialisms between states, not a struggle between savagery and civilization or between Might and Right. So the effect of the war was merely the overthrow of one imperialism by another imperialism; what survived was still imperialism.

Now we want to revive China's lost nationalism and use the strength of our four hundred millions to fight for mankind against injustice; this is our divine mission. The Powers are afraid that we will have such thoughts and are setting forth a specious doctrine. They are now advocating cosmopolitanism to inflame us, declaring that, as the civilization of the world advances and as mankind's vision enlarges, nationalism becomes too narrow, unsuited to the present age, and hence that we should espouse cosmopolitanism. In recent years led astray by this doctrine, some of China's youths, devotees of the new culture, have been opposing nationalism. But it is not a doctrine which wronged races should talk about. We, the wronged races, must first recover our position of national freedom and equality before we are fit to discuss cosmopolitanism. We must understand that cosmopolitanism grows out of nationalism; if we want to extend cosmopolitanism we must first establish strongly our own nationalism. If nationalism cannot become strong, cosmopolitanism certainly cannot prosper. Thus we see that cosmopolitanism is hidden in the heart of nationalism just as the ticket was hidden inside the bamboo pole; if we discard nationalism and go and talk cosmopolitanism we are just like the coolie who threw his bamboo pole into the sea. We put the cart before the horse.

Gentlemen, you know that revolution is naturally a thing of bloodshed. Thus, in the revolutions of T'ang* and Wu,** everyone said that the rebels were "obedient to Heaven and well-pleasing to men" but as to the fighting it was said that they experienced "battle staves floating on rivers of blood." In the Revolution of 1911, when we overthrew the Manchus, how

* First emperor of the Shang, who defeated the Hsia and became the overlord of China about 1800 B. C.

** Emperor Wu overwhelmed the Shang and began to rule the entire ancient China in 1121 B. C.

much blood was spilled? The reason for the small bloodshed then was the Chinese people's love of peace, an outstanding quality of the Chinese character. The Chinese are really the greatest lovers of peace in the world.

European superiority to China is not in political philosophy but altogether in the field of material civilization. With the progress of European material civilization, all the daily provisions for clothing, food, housing and communication have become extremely convenient and time-saving, and the weapons of war have become extraordinarily perfected and deadly. All these new inventions and weapons have come since the development of science. It was after the seventeenth and eighteenth centuries, when Bacon, Newton and other great scholars advocated the use of observation, experiment, and investigation of all things, that science came into being. So when we speak of Europe's scientific progress and of the advance of European material civilization, we are talking about something which has only two hundred years' history. A few hundred years ago, Europe could not compare with China, so now if we want to learn from Europe we should learn what we ourselves lack —science—but not political philosophy. Europeans are still looking to China for the fundamentals of political philosophy. You all know that the best schol-arship to-day is found in Germany. Yet German scholars are studying Chinese philosophy and even Indian Buddhist principles to supplement their partial conceptions of science. Cosmopolitanism has just flowered out in Europe during this generation, but it was talked of two thousand years ago in China. Europeans cannot yet discern our ancient civilization, yet many of our race have thought of a political world civilization; and as for international morality, our four hundred millions have devoted to the principle of world peace. But because of the loss of our nationalism, our ancient morality and civilization have not been able to manifest themselves and are now even declining.

The cosmopolitanism which Europeans are talking about to-day is really a principle supported by force without justice. The English expression "might is right" means that fighting for acquisition is just. The Chinese mind has never regarded acquisition by war as right; it considers aggressive warfare barbarous. This pacifist morality is the true spirit of cosmopolitanism. Upon what foundation can we defend and build up this spirit?—Upon nationalism. So we must talk nationalism first if we want to talk cosmopolitanism. "Those desiring to pacify the world must first govern their own state." Let us revive our lost nationalism and make it shine with greater splendor, then we will have some ground for discussing internationalism.

LECTURE FIVE

Delivered on February 24, 1924.

My subject to-day is: What means shall we use to revive our nationalism? If we do not find some means to recover our lost nationalism, then China will not only perish as a nation but also perhaps as a race. So, if we want to save China, we must first find a way to revive our nationalism.

To-day I shall discuss two ways by which our nationalism can be revived: the first is by awakening our four hundred millions to see where we stand. We are at a crisis when we must escape misery and seek happiness, escape death and find life. First we must see clearly and then, of course, act. China formerly did not know that she was in decline and so perished; if she had seen ahead, she might not have perished. The ancient sayings "The nation without foreign foes and outside dangers will always be ruined," and "Many adversities will revive a state" are altogether psychological truisms. "Foreign foes and outside dangers," for example: if a nation thinks that it has no outside dangers, that it is perfectly secure, that it is the strongest country in the world the foreigners will not dare to invade it, so defense is unnecessary, that nation will crumble. "Many adversities will revive a state," because, as soon as we understand what these adversities are, our energies will be aroused to heroic deeds. It is also a matter of psychology. If the situation which I have described in my first four lectures is true, then we must keep clearly in mind the perilous position which we now occupy and the critical period in which we are now living, before we can know how to revive our lost nationalism. If we attempt a revival without understanding the situation, all hope will disappear forever and the Chinese people will soon be destroyed.

Gathering up the points in my previous lectures, what are the disasters which threaten us and from what direction do they come? They come from the Great Powers, and they are: first political oppression; second, economic oppression; and third, the more rapid growth of population among the Powers. These three disasters from without are already upon our heads, and our people are in a most dangerous situation. The first disaster, the destruction of the nation by political force, may happen in a day. China, now under the political yoke of the Powers, may go to smash at any moment; we are not sure we can live from one morning to another. There are two ways in which political force can destroy a nation: through military power and through diplomacy. To see how military power can destroy a nation in a day, look at history: in the one battle of Yaimen, China of the Sung dynasty was destroyed by the Mongols; in the one battle of Yangchow the Ming dynasty fell. In foreign history, the one battle of

Waterloo was enough to overthrow the empire of Napoleon I, and the battle of Sedan to ruin the empire of Napoleon III. If, then, one battle is able to cause the downfall of a nation, China is in daily peril of her life, for our army and navy and strategic points are not prepared for defense, and foreign troops could break through at any time and defeat us.

As I just said, there have been two methods used by political powers in the destruction of states—military force and diplomacy. Military force means the use of gun and cannon, which we have some idea how to resist; diplomacy means the demolishing of China with paper and pen, which we have not learned how to counteract. Looking at the political forces which threaten a nation, China is now in a position of extreme peril.

The second disaster is the foreign economic domination which is increasing each day.

So, as I see it, if we still do not awake but go on in the way we have been going, even though the foreign diplomatists should sleep on their job, our nation would be ruined in ten years.

Then there is a third disaster which threatens us. The population of China has not increased during the past hundred years, and it will hardly increased during the next hundred years unless we find some way to stimulate the growth.

These three disasters are already upon us. We ourselves must first know the facts, we must understand that these disasters are imminent, we must broadcast them until everyone realizes what a tragedy would be our nation's downfall and with what difficulty China will escape from the perils that encompass her. When we know all these facts, what shall we do? The proverb says, "The desperate beast can yet fight." When we are driven to no place of escape, then we have to rouse our energies to a life and death struggle with our enemies. These calamities are already upon us. Can we fight? Certainly we can fight. But to be able to fight we must realize that our death hour is near. If we want to advance nationalism we must first make our four hundred millions know that their death hour is at hand, then the beset beast will still turn the fight. Do our people of the point of death want to fight? Gentlemen, you are students, soldiers, officials; you are all men of foresight and vision. You must lead our four hundred millions to see that our race is in dire peril; and if our four hundred millions understand the danger, then it will not be difficult to revive our nationalism.

Foreigners are constantly saying that the Chinese are a "sheet of loose sand"; in the matter of national sentiment it is true. We have never had national unity. Have we had any other kind of unity? As I said before, China has had exceedingly compact family and clan groups and the family and clan sentiment of the Chinese is very deep-rooted. For instance, when two Chinese meet each other on the road, they will chat together and ask each other's "honorable surname" and "great name" ;if they happen to find that they are of the same clan, they become wonderfully intimate and cordial and look upon each other as uncle or brother of the same family. If this worthy clan sentiment could be expanded, we might develop nationalism out of clanism. If we are to recover our lost nationalism, we must have some kind of group unity, large group unity. An easy and successful way to bring about the unity of a large group is to build upon the foundation of small united groups, and the small units we can build upon in China are the clan groups and also the family groups. The "native place" sentiment of the Chinese is very deep-rooted too; it is especially easy to unite those who are from the same province, prefecture or village.

As I see it, if we take these two fine sentiments as a foundation, it will be easy to bring together the people of the whole country. But to reach the desired end, it will be necessary for all to cooperate; if we can secure this cooperation, it should be easier for the Chinese to revive their nationalism than for people of other countries. For in the West the individual is the unit, and laws regarding the right of parents and children, brothers and sisters, husbands and wives, aim at the protection of the individual; in lawsuits, no questions are asked about family conditions, only the morals of the individual are considered. The individual expands immediately into the state; between the individual and the state there is no common, firm, social unit. So in welding the citizens together into a state, foreign countries do not have the advantage that China has. Because China lays emphasis upon the family as well as upon the individual, the family head has to be consulted on all matters, a system which some approve and some criticize. But I think that in the relation between the citizens of China and their state, there must first be family loyalty, then clan loyalty, and finally national loyalty. Such a system, expanding step by step, will be orderly and well regulated and the relationship between the small and the large social groups will be a real one. If we take the clans as our social units and, after improving their internal organization, join them together to form a state, our task will naturally be easier than that of foreign countries which make the individual the unit. Where the individual is the unit, there will be at least millions of units in a country, four hundred millions in China; the knitting together of such a huge number of separate units would naturally be very difficult.

But suppose we make the clan our unit: the Chinese surnames are commonly said to be only a hundred in number; different ancestors have sometimes been honored in the same clan and the number of clans has increased, yet at most there are not over four hundred to-day. All within the clan are collateral kindred; each family is constantly revising its genealogical record, pushing back its ancestry tens and hundreds of generations to the age-long past. The names of the first ancestors were often changed from other names and but few search as far back as these original surnames. This custom of tracing the ancestral line back to its earliest sources is thousands of years old and firmly rooted in Chinese social life. Foreigners think the custom a useless one, but this idea of "reverencing ancestors and being kind to the clan" has been imbedded for millenniums in the Chinese mind. So a Chinese ignored the downfall of his country; he did not care who his emperor was, and all he had to do was to pay his grain tax. But if anything was said about the possible extinction of his clan, he would be in terror lest the ancestral continuity of blood and food be broken, and he would give his life to resist that.

Let us take the clans as small foundations and work at building up the nation upon these. Suppose China has four hundred clans: it would be just as if we were working with four hundred individual people. We would make use of the original organization that each family name already has, and, in the name of the clan, begin to rally the people together, first in the neighborhood and prefecture, then in the province, and finally throughout the country, until each family name had become a large united group. For instance, if all members bearing the surname of Chen using the original organization as a basis, would rally together all those who bore the same surname in their neighborhood and prefecture, then in the province, within two or three years, I think, the Chen clan would become a very large body. When every clan was so organized upon a very large scale, we would next unite the clans that had some connection with each other to form larger groups, and we would make every group know that great disasters threaten us, that our death hour is approaching, but that if we all combined, we could become a great national union—the Republic of China—and that with such a union we need not fear outside adversaries or our inability to revive the state. If we start with our four hundred million individual citizens instead of with our four hundred clans, we will not know where to begin in consolidating the sheet of loose sand.

If all our people know that they are oppressed citizens, that we have come to a time when we are simply up against it, that if we combine we must first organize the various clans into clan groups and then these clan groups into a great national union, we will have some positive methods with which to combat the foreigner. As it is, we cannot fight because we have no united group; if we had, resistance would be easy. China is not at the present moment destroyed; the common people, though they may not easily perform other tasks, can do such things as these—refuse to work for foreigners, refuse to be foreign slaves or to use foreign goods manufactured abroad, push the use of native goods, decline to use foreign bank notes, use only Chinese government money, and sever economic relations with foreigners. The other problem of population growth will be easily solved; China's population has always been large and her resources abundant, and our past oppression can be attributed to the ignorance of the masses, who "live in a stupor and die in a dream." If our whole body of citizens can realize a great national unity upon the basis of our clan groups, no matter what pressure foreign nations bring upon us—military, economic, or population—we will not fear. So the fundamental way to save China from her imminent destruction is for us first to attain unity. If three or four hundred clan groups will take thought for the state, there will be a way out for us and, no matter what nation we face, we will be able to resist.

There are two ways of resisting a foreign Power. The first is the positive way—arousing the nation spirit, and seeking solutions for the problems of democracy and livelihood. The second way is the negative way—non-cooperation and passive resistance—whereby foreign imperialistic activity is weakened, the national standing is defended, and nation destruction is averted.

LECTURE SIX

Delivered on March 2, 1924.

Gentlemen: My subject to-day is: How can we restore the standing of our nation? In studying this question we must not forget what has been said in the previous lectures. What is the present standing of our nation? What is the situation of our nation and state in the world of to-day?

Why did China once occupy so exalted a place and then "fall ten thousand feet in one drop"? The chief cause I have already discussed with you: because we lost our national spirit, our state has day by day degenerated. So if we want to restore our national standing, we must first revive our national spirit. If we want to revive our national spirit, we must fulfill two conditions. First, we must understand that we occupy to-day a most perilous position; and second, knowing our danger, we must utilize China's ancient social groups, as the family and the clan, and consolidate them to form a great national body. When this is accomplished and we have the strength of four hundred millions united to fight, no matter how low our present position, we should be able to lift it up. So, to know and to unite are the two essentials for reviving our nationalism. When all of you have come to understand these essentials, you must proclaim them among the four hundred millions of the whole country until everybody understands them. Then we can begin to revive our lost national spirit. Our old national spirit is asleep; we must awake it and then our nationalism will begin to revive. When our nationalism is revived, we can go a step farther and study how to restore our national standing.

China did not reach her former position of greatness by one road only. Usually a nation becomes strong at first by the expansion of its military power, then by the development of various forms of culture; but if the nation and the state are to maintain a permanent standing, moral character is essential. Only by attaining a high standard of morality can the state hope to govern long and exist at peace. Because the character of the Chinese race was higher than that of other races, the Mongols, although they conquered China during the Sung dynasty, were later absorbed by the Chinese; and the Manchus, although China of the Ming dynasty fell twice before them, were assimilated by the Chinese. Because of the high moral standards of our race, we have been able not only to survive in spite of the downfall of the state, but we have had power to assimilate these outside races. So, coming to the root of the matter, if we want to restore our race's standing, besides uniting all into a great national body, we must first recover our ancient morality then, and only then, can we plan how to attain again to the national position we once held.

As for China's old moral standards, they are not yet lost sight of by the people of China. First come Loyalty and Filial Devotion, then Kindness and Love, the Faithfulness and Justice, then Harmony and Peace. The Chinese still speak of these ancient qualities of character. But since our domination by alien races and since the invasion of foreign culture which has spread its influence all over China, a group intoxicated with the new culture have begun to reject the old morality, saying that the former makes the latter unnecessary. They do not understand that we ought to preserve what is good in our past and throw away only the bad. China now is in a period of conflict between old and new currents and a large number of our people have nothing to follow after.

A few days ago I was in the country and entered an ancestral temple. On going to the innermost court to rest, I saw on the right-hand side the character for "Filial Devotion", but on the left side a blank where there must have been previously, I think, the character for "Loyalty."* This I have seen more than once; many ancestral or family temples are in the same condition. But the character for "Filial Devotion," which I observed the other day, was extra large, while the marks on the left wall where the character had been scratched off looked very recent. It may have been the work of the country folk themselves or of soldiers living in the temple, yet I have seen many ancestral temples which had not been billets for soldiers with the character for "Loyalty" rubbed off the walls. This shows the thinking of a certain type of people to-day: because we have a republic, we need not talk about loyalty. They say that in former days loyalty was shown to princes, and that as there

* Filial Devotion, *hsiao,* and loyalty, *chung,* are constantly associated being considered attributes of the same virtue. When manifested in the relationship between father and son, it is *hsiao,* when manifested in the relationship beween emperor and officers, it is *chung.*

are no princes in democracy, so loyalty is not needed and can be cast aside. Such an argument is certainly due to misunderstanding: we do not want princes in the country, but we do cannot do without loyalty. If we say that loyalty is outworn to-day, what about the nation? Can we not direct our loyalty towards the nation? Of course we cannot now speak of loyalty to princes, but how about loyalty to the people and loyalty to our tasks? When we undertake a task we should not falter from first to last until the task is done; if we do not succeed, we should not begrudge our very lives as a sacrifice—this is loyalty. The ancient teaching of loyalty pushed to its limit meant death. To say that ancient loyalty was due to kings and, since now we have no kings, we do not need loyalty and can do as we please, is absolutely wrong. Now everybody who talks about democracy breaks down all the old moral standards, and the fundamental reason is right here. In a democracy it stands to reason what we should still show loyalty, not to princes but to nation and to the people. Loyalty to four hundred millions must naturally be on a much higer level than loyalty to one individual; so I say that the fine moral quality of loyalty must still be cherished.

Filial Devotion is even more a characteristic of China, and we have gone far beyond other nations in the practice of it. Filial duty as revealed in the "Canon of Filial Piety" covers almost the whole field of human activity, touching every point; there is no treatise on filial piety in any civilized country to—day that is so complete. Filial Devotion is still indispensable. If the people of the democracy can carry out Loyalty and Filial Devotion to the limit, our state will naturally flourish.

Kindness and Love are also part of China's high morality. In past no one discussed love better than Motze.* His "love without discrimination" is the same thing as Jesus' "universal love." The ancients applied the principle of love

* Often spelt as Mao Tzu, a comtemporary of Confucius.

to government, saying, "Love the people as your children," and, "Be kind to all the people and love all creatures." Love was used to embrace all duties, from which we can see how well they put kindness and love into effect. Since our foreign intercourse began, some people have thought that the Chinese ideal of kindness and love was inferior to the foreigners' because foreigners in China, by establishing schools and carrying on hospital to teach and relieve the Chinese, have been practicing kindness and love. In the practical expression of the fine qualities of kindness and love, it does seem as though China were far behind other countries, and the reason is that the Chinese have been less active in performance. Yet Kindness and Love are old qualities of Chinese character, and as we study other countries, let us learn their practical methods, revive our own kindness and love, the spirit of ancient China, and make them shine with greater glory.

Faithfulness and Justice. Ancient China

always spoke of Faithfulness in dealing with neighboring countries and in intercourse with friends. In my estimation, the quality of faithfulness is practiced better by Chinese than by foreigners. This can be seen in business intercourse: Chinese in their business relations do not use written contracts; all that is necessary is a verbal promise which is implicitly trusted. Thus, when a foreigner places an order for goods with a Chinese, no contract is necessary; there is simply an entry on the books and the bargain is closed. As a result, foreigners who have done business for a long time in the interior of China invariably speak highly of the Chinese, saying that a Chinese will keep his word better than a foreigner his contract.

Justice. China in her mightiest days never utterly destroyed another state. Look at Korea, which was formerly a tributary of China in name, but an independent nation in reality. China was a strong state for thousands of years and Korea lived on; Japan has been a strong state for not over twenty years and Korea is already destroyed. From this one can see that Japan's sense of "faithfulness and justice" is inferior to China's and that China's standards have advanced beyond those of other nations.

China has one more splendid virtue—the love of Harmony and Peace. Among the states and the peoples of the world to-day China alone preaches peace; other countries all talk in terms of war and advocate the overthrow of states by imperialism. The intense love of peaces which the Chinese have had these thousands of years has been a natural disposition. In individual relationships great stress has been laid upon "humility and deference"; in government the old saying was, "He who delights not in killing a man can unify all men." All of this is very different from the ideals of foreigners. China's ancients virtues of Loyalty, Filial Devotion, Kindness, Love, Faithfulness, and such are in their very nature superior to foreign virtues, but in the moral quality of Peace we will further surpass the people of other lands. This special characteristic is the spirit of our nation and we must not only cherish it but cause it to shine with greater luster; then our national standing will be restored.

We must revive not only our old morality but also our old learning. If we want to regain our national spirit, we must reawaken the learning as well as the moral ideals which we once possessed. What is this ancient learning? Among the human theories of the state, China's political philosophy holds a high place. We think that the states of Europe and America have made great strides forward in recent years, yet their new culture is not so complete as our old political philosophy. China has a specimen of political philosophy so systematic and so clear that nothing has been discovered or spoken by foreign statesmen to equal it. It is found in the "Great Learning": "Search into the nature of things, extend the boundaries of knowledge, make the purpose sincere, regulate the mind, cultivate personal virtue, rule the family, govern the state, pacify the world." This calls upon a man to deyelop from within outward, to begin with his inner nature and not cease until the world is at peace. Such a deep, all-embracing logic is not found in or spoken by any foreign political philosopher; it is a nugget of wisdom peculiar to China's philosophy of state and worthy to be preserved.

The principles of "regulating the mind, making sincere the purpose, cultivating personal virtue, ruling the family," naturally belong in the field of morals, but to-day it will be more fitting to treat them as matters of knowledge. Although our forefathers exercised their powers on the moral side, since the loss of our nationalism the true spirit of learning has likewise disappeared. The common people who study the classics constantly use the passage that I quoted in a conventional way, but they repeat the words without seeking their interpretation and with no idea of their deeper meaning. The knowledge of how to "regulate the mind and make sincere the purpose" springs from inward control and is difficult to expound. The scholars of the Sung* Period paid much attention to this mental training, and as we study their books, we can see how well they succeeded. But the "cultivation of personal virtue, ruling the family, governing the state," are outward reforms which wc have not yet effected; on the surface, at least, we have not succeeded in any of them for the past hundreds of years. As a result, we cannot govern our own country, and foreigners, seeing we cannot do so, want to come and establish international control over us.

Why can we not govern China? What reveals the fact to foreigners? In my personal opinion, foreigners have no way of observing whether we rule our families well or not, but they can see that we are very much lacking in personal culture. Every word and act of a Chinese shows absence of refinement; one con-

* The Sung Dynasty 960-1127 A.D.

tact with Chinese people is enough to reveal this.

Confucius said, "If the mat is not straight, do not sit down,"* which shows how much attention he paid to personal culture even to the minute details of sitting and standing. The Confucian scholars of the Sung age were even more careful and strict in "regulating the mind, making the purpose sincere, and cultivating the person," but modern Chinese hardly give these matters a thought. As a result, although we have the wisdom about "cultivating personal virtue, regulating the family, governing the state, pacifying the world," as soon as foreigners meet us, they say that we are barbaric and they will not study deeply into our learning. With the exception of philosophers like Russell, no foreigners can at first sight of China understand her civilization, and only those who have spent ten or more years in China can appreciate her age-long culture. If

* In the plain language of modern times, it is a matter of table etiquette.

everyone would devote some systematic effort to the culture of his person, "let the character within be manifested without," pay attention to even the smallest matters of conduct, on meeting foreigners not rudely trespass upon their freedom, then foreigners would certainly respect the Chinese. That is why I am speaking to-day on personal culture. You young men should certainly learn from the modern culture of foreigners and first cultivate your own persons, then you can talk about "ruling families and governing the state." Government is progressing in every other country to-day; in China it is going backward. Why? Because we are under the political and economic domination of foreign nations, yes; but if we search for the fundamental reason, we will find it in the Chinese failure to cultivate personal virtue. We seem to forget that the ancients of China related personal culture back to "regulating the mind, making sincere the purpose, searching into the nature of things, and extending the boundaries of knowledge." What discriminating teaching, what comprehensive philosophy! And it is China's ancient wisdom. If now we want to rule our families and govern our state and not be subject to foreign control, we must begin with personal culture, we must revive China's ancient wisdom and comprehensive philosophy, and then we can reawaken the spirit and restore the standing of the Chinese nation.

In addition to our ancient learning there are likewise our ancient powers. When the Chinese to-day see the development of foreign machinery and glorious progress of modern science, they naturally think that our ability is not equal to the ability of foreigners. But what about the capabilities of the Chinese thousands of years ago? In olden the Chinese were much superior to foreigners. Some of the most valued things in the West to-day were invented in ancient China. Take, for example, the compass, which, in this great age of shipping, cannot be dispensed with for an hour or a moment; we find that it was invented by the

Chinese millenniums ago. Chinese could not have invented the compass without some sort of ability, and that foreigners are still using what China used in the distant past shows that the Chinese ability is superior. There is another thing which occupies an extremely important place in civilization the art of printing. The modern improved printing press of the West can turn out tens of thousands of newspapers in an hour, yet the history of printing begins with early Chinese inventions. Take, again, porcelain ware, which makind uses daily, another invention and special product of China; foreigners are still trying to imitate it but cannot match its delicacy and beauty. In modern wars smokeless powder is used, yet this is only an improvement upon the smoke-producing black gunpowder which was invented by the Chinese. These important and valuable inventions—the compass, printing, gunpowder—are known and used by Western nations to-day and are reasons for their greatness.

In the field of human food and clothing, shelter and communication, China has also contributed many discoveries for the use of mankind. Take beverages: China discovered the tea leaf, which is one of the great necessities in the modern world; civilized countries today compete in the use of it and are making it a substitute for liquors. Thus tea is helping in the eradication of the drink evil and is bringing not a few other benefits to mankind. Take clothing: foreigners place the highest value upon articles made of silk and wearers of silk garments are daily increasing; the silkworm which spins the silk was first found in China thousands of years ago. Or shelter: the modern houses built by foreigners are of course complete in every way but the principles of building and all the important parts of house were first devised by the Chinese. The arched doorway, for example, was introduced earlier in China than anywhere else. Study methods of communication: Westerners think that their suspension bridges are extremely modern engineering and the result of great native ability, but foreigners who visit the interior of China and reach the borders of Szechwan and Tibet see Chinese traversing high mountains and crossing deep rivers by means of suspension bridges. They then realize that the credit for inventing suspension bridges belongs to China and not to the West as they had thought. All this goes to show that ancient China was not without capabilities, but these powers were afterwards lost, and consequently our national position has declined. If we want to restore our former standing, we must also revive our ancient powers.

But even if we succeed in reviving our ancient morality, learning and powers, will still not be able, in this modern world, to advance China to a first place among the nations. If we can reproduce the best of our national heritage just as it was in the time of our fore-fathers when China dominated the world, we will still need to learn the strong points of Europe and America before we progress at equal rate with them. Unless we do study the best from foreign countries we will go backward. With our own fine foundation of knowledge and our age-long culture, with our own native intelligence besides, we should be able to acquire all the best things from abroad. The strongest point of the West is its science. This has been three hundred years in the course of development, but it has made rapid strides forward only within the last half century. The advance of science has made it possible for man to "usurp the powers of nature" and to do what natural forces had done.

The most recently discovered natural power is electricity. Formerly power was gotten from coal, which in trun generated machine power. Now Western science has advanced to the second age—the age of electricity. There is a tremendous project on foot in the United States to link up all the electrical horse power of the factories throughout the country into one unified system. Since there are thousands of factories, if each one has its own generating plant and burns its own coal to generate electric power, an enormous amount of coal and labor is used. Because of this heavy consumption of coal by the factories, the hundreds of thousands of miles of railroad are not sufficient to transport the needed fuel. The result is that the railways are too busy to move the agricultural products of the various sections, and these do not find the wide market they should. Since the use of coal has two such serious disadvantages, the United States is now considering a great central power station which would unite the electric power used by the thousands of factories into one system. If this super-power project succeeds, then all the generating equipment of the thousands of factories can be consolidated into one central plant. The individual factory will not need to use coal and a lot of laborers to feed the fires; all it will need to carry on its work will be a copper wire to conduct the power. The advantages of this plan may be illustrated by the hundreds of people gathered in this lecture hall. If each one of us should have a small stove to cook a meal here, it would be troublesome and wasteful, but if all joined together and cooked a meal on a big stove, we would find it much more convenient and economical. The United States is just considering this scheme of linking together all its factories in one great electric power system; if China wants to learn the strong points of the West, she should not start with coal power but with electricity, and give a single, great motive power to the whole country. This way of learning may be compared to what military men call a frontal attack, "intercepting and striking at the advance force." If we can learn from the advance guard, within ten years we may not be ahead of other nations, but we will be keeping step with them.

If we want to learn from the West, we will have to catch up with the advance line and not chase from behind. In the study of science, for instance, this will mean the saving of two hundred years. We are in such a position to-day that if we should still slumber on, not commence to struggle, and not know how to restore the standing of our state, our country would be lost and our race wiped out forever. But now that we know how, we ought to follow the world currents and study the best features of Western nations; we certainly should go beyond other countries in what we study and cause the "last to be first." Although we went backward for many centuries, yet now it should take us but a few years to catch up with the rest of the world. Japan is a good example. Her culture was formerly copied from China and was much inferior to ours, but recently Japan has studied only European and American civilization and within a few decades has become one of the world's great powers. I do not think that our intellectual powers are below those of the Japanese, and it should be easier for us now than for Japan to learn from the West. So the next ten years is a critical period for us; if we can come to life as the Japanese did and all put forth a very sincere effort to elevate the standing of our nation, within a decade we able to get rid of foreign political and economic control, the pressure of foreign population increase, and all the various calamities that are now upon us.

After China reaches that place, what then? A common phrase in ancient China was, "Rescue the weak, lift up the fallen." Because of this noble policy China prospered for thousands of years, and Annam, Burma, Korea, Siam, and other small states were able to maintain their independence. As European influence spread over the East, Annam was overthrown by France, Burma by Great Britain, Korea by Japan. If we want China to rise to power, we must not only restore our national standing, but we must also assume a great responsibility towards the world. If China cannot assume that responsibility, she will be a great disadvantage not an advantage to the world, no matter how strong she may be. What really is our duty to the world? The road which the Great Powers are traveling to-day means the destruction of other states; if China, when she becomes strong, wants to crush other countries, copy the Powers' imperialism, and go their road, we will just be following in their tracks. Let us first of all decide on our policy. Only if we "rescue the weak and lift up the fallen" will we be carrying out the divine obligation of our nation. We must aid weaker and smaller peoples and oppose the great powers of the world. If all the people of the country resolve upon this purpose, our nation will prosper; otherwise, there is no hope for us. Let us to-day, before China's development begins, pledge ourselves to lift up the fallen and to aid the weak; then when we become strong and look back upon our own sufferings under the political and economic domination of the Powers and see weaker and smaller peoples undergoing similar treatment, we will rise and smite that imperialism. Then will we be truly "governing the state and pacifying the world."

If we want to be able to reach this ideal in

the future, we must now revive our national spirit, recover our national standing, unify the world upon the foundation of our ancient morality and love of peace, and bring about a universal rule of equality and fraternity. This is the great responsibility which develop upon our four hundred millions. You, gentlemen, are a part of our four hundred millions; you must all shoulder this responsibility and manifest the true spirit of our nation.

THE PRINCIPLE OF DEMOCRACY

LECTURE ONE

Delivered on March 9, 1924.

What is the People's Sovereignty? In order to define this term we must first understand what a "people" is. Any unified and organized body of men is called a "people." What is "sovereignty"? It is power and authority extended to the area of the state. The states with the greatest power to-day are called in Chinese the "strong states," in foreign languages the "powers." Mechanical force is spoken of in Chinese as "horse strength," in other languages as "horse power." Thus strength and power are used interchangeably. The power to execute orders and to regulate public conduct is called "sovereignty," and when "people" and "sovereignty" are linked together, we have the political power of the people. To understand "political power" we must know what government is. Many people think that government is a very abstruse and difficult subject which ordinary persons cannot comprehend. Chinese military men are always saying, "We are soldiers and know nothing about politics." The reason why they are ignorant is that they consider government to be a deep and abstruse study. They do not know that it is a very clear and comprehensible thing. If military men say that they will not interfere with government, we can let them by; but if they say that they cannot understand government; they are foolish. Since the soldier is the driving force behind the government, he should certainly understand what government is. Briefly, government is a thing of the people and by the people; it is control of the affairs of all the people. The power of control is political sovereignty, and where the people control the government we speak of the "people's sovereignty."

Now that we understand what the "people's sovereignty" is, we must study its functions. As we view life about us or study into the distant past, we see that human power has been employed, to put it simply, in maintaining the existence of the human race. In order to exist, mankind must have protection and sustenance and it is daily engaged in meeting these two great needs. Protection means self-defense: whether it is an individual or a group or a state, the power of self-defense is necessary to existence. Sustenance means seeking food. Self-defense and food-seeking are, then, the two chief means by which mankind maintains its existence. But while man is maintaining his existence, other animals are also trying to maintain theirs; while man is defending himself, other animals are also defending themselves; while man seeks food, other animals are also seeking food; and so the protection and the sustenance of man comes into conflict with the protection and the sustenance of other animals, and struggle ensues. To keep alive in the midst of struggle man must fight, and so mankind has not ceased to fight since the beginning of human life. Thus the human race has used its strength in combat, and since its birth upon the planet until now has lived in the thick of strife.

While the germs of democracy were found in Greece and Rome two thousand years ago, yet only within the last one hundred fifty years has democracy become firmly rooted in the world. The preceding age was one of autocracy and the age before that one of theocracy. Before theocracy came the wilderness age when men fought with beasts. Man sought to live and the animal sought to live. Man had two ways of preserving his existence—through seeking food and through self-defense. In very ancient times men ate beasts and beasts also ate men; there was a constant struggle between them. The land was covered with venomous snakes and wild animals; man was beset by dangers and so had to fight for his very life. The warfare of that day was the irregular conflict between man and beast; there was no banding into groups, it was "each fighting for himself."

In the primitive struggle between man and wild beasts, man used only his individual physical strength or sometimes the species would fight together; if, for instance, in one place a few score men were battling with a few score beasts, and in another place, another group of men were doing the same thing, the men of both places might perceive their own kinship to each other and their difference from the animals, unite as fellow creatures, and fight together against the other species. Certainly man would not join with another species to fight and devour man and injure his own kind. Such a banding together of the species and unwitting alliance against reptiles and beasts was a natural, not an artificial thing; when the reptiles or beasts were destroyed, the men scattered. At that time there was no such thing as popular sovereignty; man, in fighting the animals, used simply his own physical prowess and not any kind of authority. It was an age of brute force.

Later, when man had about exterminated the venomous reptiles and savage beasts, when his environment was somewhat improved, and his dwelling place was better suited to his type of existence, then groups of people began to live in one place and to domesticate the tamer animals. This was the beginning of the pastoral age and also of civilization. A great change now took place in man's living conditions: warfare with animals was about at an end, civilization was growing up, what we call the ancient period of human history had arrived. Man began to direct his warfare against the forces of Nature. Briefly, in the first stage man warred with beasts and employed his own brute force or the united strength of many to kill them off; in the second stage man warred with Nature. In the first stage, because man did not know when an animal would attack him, he was not sure whether he could live from one moment to another; he had only his two hands and two feet for self-defense, but he was wiser than the beasts and learned to use sticks and stones for weapons, so finally he won a complete victory over his wild enemies. Only then could man plan ahead for a day; while he was battling with the beasts, his life was not secure for a moment.

When wild beasts no longer threatened, the human race began to multiply and the most favorable spots on the earth began to fill up with people. What were the favorable spots?—Places sheltered from wind and rain or regions which storms did not touch.

After driving out the poisonous reptiles and savage beasts they were faced with natural disasters of storm and flood. Naturally they would try to avert these disasters and to struggle against Nature. In the age of warfare with the beasts man could use his own physical strength to fight, but mere fighting was of no value in the day of struggle against Nature. Mankind then suffered many hardships until some wise men came forth with schemes for the welfare of the people. Thus the Great Yü* reduced the waters to order and averted the calamity of flood for the people, and Yu Ch'ao Shih (the Nest Builder)** taught the people how to build houses in trees and avert the disasters from wind and storm.

From this time on civilization slowly progressed, the people began to unite, and, as land was plentiful and the inhabitants were few, food was very easy to procure. The only problems were the catastrophes of Nature which could not be fought, as the wild beasts were, with bodily strength, and so there arose the idea of divine power. Men of deep wisdom began to advocate the doctrine of gods and divine teachings, and introduced prayers as a means of warding off evil and obtaining blessings. There was no way of telling at the time whether their praying was effective or not; however, since they were stuggling against Heaven, they had no other plan, when in ex-

* The first emperor of the Hsia.

** Legendary ruler of ancient Chinese history.

tremity, but to appeal for the power of the gods. A man of profound insight would be chosen as leader, like the chiefs of savage tribes in Africa to-day, whose special duty it was to offer prayers. In the same way Mongolians and Tibetans now make a "Living Buddha" their ruler and are under a religious government. So the ancients used to say that the two great functions of the state were worship and war, praying and fighting.

Thus after the age of warfare with wild animals came the struggles with Nature and out of these struggles was born theocracy. The next step in history was autocracy, when mighty warriors and political leaders wrested the power away from the religious rulers or put themselves at the head of the churches and appointed themselves kings. A period of struggle between man and man thus evolved. When struggles between man and man began to take the place of struggles with Nature, people realized that simple dependence upon the power of religious faith could neither protect society nor aid in warfare and that an enlightened government and strong military power were necessary in order to compete with other peoples. Men have fought against men since the beginning of recorded history. At first they employed both the power of religion and the power of autocracy in their struggles; later, as theocracy weakened and, after the dissolution of the Roman Empire, gradually decayed, autocracy became stronger until, in the reign of Louis XIV of France, it reached the peak of its power. Louis XIV said that there was no difference between the king and the state—"I am the king, therefore I am the state." He took every power of the state into his own hands and exercised despotism to its limits, just as did Ch'in Shih Hwang* of China. The absolute monarchy became more terrible every day until the people could bear it no longer. About this time science was beginning to make steady progress and the general

* Despot who united China and founded the Ch'in dynasty (246–207 B.C.)

intelligence of mankind was steadily rising. As a result, a new consciousness was born. The people saw that autocracy was something that only grasped for power, made private property of the state and of the people, contributed to the gratification of one individual and did not care about the sufferings of the many; as it became unbearable, they realized with increasing clearness that, since the system was iniquitous. they should resist it, and that resistance meant revolution. So, during the last hundred years, the tides of revolutionary thought have run high and have given rise to democratic revolutions, struggles between people and kings.

This division into periods will help us in studying the origins of democracy. Summing up: the first period was one of struggle between man and beast in which man employed physical strength rather than any kind of power; in the second period man fought with Nature and called divine powers to his aid; in the third period, men came into conflict with men, states with states, races with races, and autocratic power was the chief weapon. We are now in the fourth period, of war within states, when the people are battling against their monarchs and kings. The issue now is between good and evil, between right and might, and as the power of the people is steadily increasing, we may call this the age of the people's sovereignty—the age of democracy. This is a very new age. We have only recently entered upon it and overthrown the autocracy of the old age.

Is the change a good thing or not? When the masses were unenlightened and depended upon sacred kings and virtuous sages to lead them, autocracy was of considerable value. Before autocracies arose, holy men founded religion upon the way of the gods in order to conserve social values; at that time theocracy rendered a large service. But now autocracy and theocracy are things of the past and we have come to the age of democracy, the age of the people's power. Is there any just reason why we should oppose autocracy and insist upon democracy? Yes, because with the rapid advance of civilization people are growing in intelligence and developing a new consciousness of self, just as we, who as children wanted our parents to support us, cannot depend upon them further but must be independent when we grow up to manhood and seek our own living.

From two hundred thousand years up to ten or more thousand years ago, mankind lived under theocracy, and theocracy was well suited to the needs of the age. The situation in Europe was a similar one a thousand or more years ago. Chinese culture flowered earlier than European culture, so we have had more autocracy than theocracy; the age of autocracy began long ago in China. But the word democracy popular sovereignty has only lately been introduced into China. All of you who have come here to-day to support my revolution are naturally believers in democracy.

Which, autocracy or democracy, is really

better suited to modern China? If we base our judgment upon the intelligence and the ability of the Chinese people, we come to the conclusion that the sovereignty of the people would be far more suitable for us. Confucius and Mencius two thousand years ago spoke for people's rights. Confucius said, "When the Great Doctrine prevails, all under heaven will work for the common good."* He was pleading for a free and fraternal world in which the people would rule. He was constantly referring to Yao and Shun** simply because they did not try to monopolize the empire. Although their government was autocratic in name, yet in reality they gave the people power and so were highly reverenced by Confucius. Mencius said, "Most precious are the people; next come the land and grain; and last, the princes." Again: "Heaven sees as the people see, Heaven hears as the people hear," and "I have heard of the

* 天下爲公 t'ien hsia wei kung

** Legendary rulers of ancient Chinese history before Great Yu.

punishment of the tyrant Chou* but never of the assassination of a sovereign." He, in his age, already saw that kings were not absolutely necessary and would not last forever, so he called those who brought happiness to the people holy monarchs, but those who were cruel and unprincipled he called individualists whom all should oppose. Thus China more than two millenniums ago had already considered the idea of democracy, but at that time she could not put it into operation. Democracy was then what foreigners call a Utopia, an ideal which could not be immediately realized.

Now that Europe and America have founded republics and have applied democracy for one hundred fifty years, we whose ancients dreamed of these things should certainly follow the tide of world events and make use of the people's power if we expect our state to rule long and peacefully and our people to enjoy

* Last ruler of the Shang or Yin dynasty which fell 1121 B. C. a cruel tyrant condemned by all Chinese historians.

happiness. But the rise of democracy is comparatively recent and many states in the world are still autocratic; those which have tried democracy have experienced many disappointments and failures. While democracy was discoursed upon in China two thousand years ago, it has become an accomplished fact for only one hundred fifty years in the West. Now it is suddenly spreading over the whole world on the wings of the wind.

The first instance of actual democracy in modern times was in England. A revolution of the people took place about the time of the close of the Ming dynasty and the beginning of the Manchu dynasty in China, under a leader named Cromwell, which resulted in the execution of King Charles I. This deed sent a thrill of horror through the people of Europe and America, who had never heard of the like in the world before and who thought that those responsible should be treated as traitors and rebels. The secret assassination of princes was common in every country, but Cromwell's execution of Charles I was not done in secret; the king was given a public trial and openly proclaimed guilty of disloyalty to the state and to the people, and so deserving of death. Europe thought that the English people would defend the rights of the people, and give a great impetus to democracy, but, to the surprise of all, the English preferred autocracy to democracy; although Charles I was dead, they continued to long for a king. Within less than ten years the restoration of the monarchy had taken place and Charles II was welcomed back as king. This happened just at the time when the Manchus were entering the Great Wall, before the downfall of the Ming dynasty* not much further back than two hundred or more years. Something over two centuries ago, England had this one period of democratic government, but it soon collapsed and autocracy again held sway.

A hundred years later the American Revolution took place when the colonies broke

* 1403–1644 A.D.

away from England and declared independence, forming the federal government of the United States of America. This state, which has now existed for one hundred fifty years, was the first in the modern world to carry out the principles of democracy. Ten years after the establishment of the American Republic, the French Revolution was precipitated. The situation at the time of the French Revolution was like this: Since Louis XIV had seized all the power of the state and exercised absolute despotism, the people of France had suffered untold miseries; when his heirs displayed an even greater cruelty and wickedness, the people were goaded beyond endurance and started to revolt. They killed Louis XVI just as the English had killed Charles I, after giving him a public trial and proclaiming his disloyalty to the state and to the people. But then all the other states of Europe arose to avenge the death of the French king and war was fought for over ten years, with the result that the revolution failed and monarchy lifted its head once more. From this time on, however, democratic ideas flourished all the more among the French people.

Everyone who discusses the history of democracy knows about the French philosopher Rousseau, who advocated popular rights in an extreme form and whose democratic theories generated the French Revolution. Rousseau's most important work out of his lifelong thinking and writing upon democracy was his *Social Contract*. The idea upon which the book is built is this: Man is born with rights of freedom and equality, rights which were endowed by Nature but which he has thrown away. According to his theory, the people are given their sovereign rights by Nature; but, as we study the evolution of history, we see that democracy has not been Heaven-born but has been wrought out of the conditions of the times and the movement of events. We can find no facts in the evolution of the race to bear out Rousseau's philosophy, which, consequently, lacks foundation. Opponents of democracy take Rousseau's unfounded arguments as material for their case, but we who believe in democracy do not need to start with discussion about it; universal principles are all based first upon fact and then upon theory, theory does not precede fact.

The theory in Rousseau's *Social Contract* that the rights and the powers of the people are bestowed by Nature is fundamentally in conflict with the principle of historical evolution, and so the enemies of democracy have used Rousseau's unsound argument to stop the mouths of the supporters of democracy. Rousseau's idea that democracy is naturally endowed was unreasonable, but for opponents to use one false conclusion of his as an argument against all democracy is just as unreasonable. When we are studying the truths of the universe, we must begin by investigating the facts and not depend merely upon the treatises of scholars. Why, if Rousseau's philosophy was not based upon fact, did all the peoples welcome it? And how was Rousseau able to produce such a treatise? He saw the power of the people rising into a flood and espoused the people's sovereignty; his democratic proposals suited the psychology of the time and made the masses welcome him. So, although his theory of democracy conflicted with the principles of historical progress, the spirit of democracy which was already coming to be a reality in the life of his day caused him to be warmly received in spite of his faulty arguments. And it may be added that Rousseau's advocacy of the original idea of democracy was one of the greatest contributions to government in all history.

Since the beginning of human history, the kind of power which government has wielded has inevitably varied according to the circumstances and tendencies of the age. In an age which reverenced gods, theocratic power had to be used; in an age of princes autocratic power had to be used. But now the currents of the world's life have swept into the age of democracy and it behooves us quickly to study what democracy means. Because some of the treatises upon democracy, such as Rousseau's *Social Contract,* have been a bit inconsistent with true principles, is no reason why we should oppose all that is good in democracy as well. Nor must we think that democracy is impracticable because the monarchy was restored after Cromwell's revolution in England or because the revolution stretched out for so long a time in France. The French Revolution lasted eighty years before it succeeded. The American Revolution accomplished its aims in eight years, but England after two hundred years of revolution still has a king. However, if we observe the steady progress of the world from many angles, we are assured that the day of democracy is here; and that, no matter what disappointments and defeats democracy may meet, it will maintain itself for a long time to come upon the earth.

Thirty years ago, therefore, we fellow revolutionists firmly resolved that, if we wanted China to be strong and our revolution to be effective, we must espouse the cause of democracy. Those Chinese who opposed democracy used to ask what strength there was in our Revolutionary Party to be able to overthrow the Manchu emperor. But in 1911 he fell with one push, another victim of the world tide. This world tendency has flowed from theocracy on to autocracy and from autocracy now on to democracy, and there is no way to stem the current. Autocracy in Europe is on the wane. Great Britain uses a political party rather than a king to govern the country; it may be called a republic with a king. From all this we see that not only theocracy but also autocracy will soon crumble before the onflowing world current. The present age of democracy is a sequence of the democratic ideas in the Greek and Roman age and, while it has been only one hundred fifty years since the beginnings of democracy, its future will be growing brighter day by day.

So we in our revolution have chosen democracy, first, that we may be following the world current, and second, that we may reduce the period of civil war. From ancient times in China, men of great ambition have all wanted to be king. Thus, when Liu Pang* saw Ch'in Shih Hwang riding out, he said, "That is the way for men of valor!" and Hsiang Yu** also said, "Let me usurp his place!" From one generation to another, there has been no end to this unscrupulous greed for power. When I launched the revolution, six or seven out of every ten who came to our support had imperialistic ideas, but after we made it known that our revolutionary principles aimed not only at the overthrow of the Manchus but also at the establishment of a republic, this group gradually got rid of their selfish ambitions. But there are still a few among them who, even in this thirteenth year of the Republic, cling to the old hope of becoming king, and this is the reason why even among our followers there were some who fought against each oth-

* The founder of the Han dynasty (204 B.C.–219 A.D.).

** A rival of Liu Pang.

er. When we first proclaimed our revolution, we lifted up the rights of the people as the basis upon which to build our republic, with the hope that this would prevent the rivalry for imperial power.

To-day I am speaking about the people's sovereignty and I want you all to understand clearly what it really means. Unless we do understand clearly, we can never get rid of imperial ambitions among us, ambitions which will make even brethren in a cause and citizens of the same country fight one another. The whole land will be torn year after year with civil strife and there will be no end to the sufferings of the people. Because I wanted us to avert such calamities, I lifted up the banner of democracy as soon as the revolution began and determined that we should found a republic. When we have a real republic, who will be king? The people, our four hundred millions, will be king. This will prevent everybody from struggling for power and will reduce the war evil in China. The history of China shows that every change of dynasty has meant war. A peaceful period has always been followed by disorder, disorder over the rivalry for kingship. Foreign countries have had wars over religion and wars over freedom, but China in her thousands of years has had but one kind of war, the war for the throne. In order to avert further civil war, we, as soon as we launched our revolution, proclaimed that we wanted a republic and not kings.

LECTURE TWO

Delivered on March 16, 1924.

Foreign scholars always associate "democracy" with "liberty" and many foreign books and essays discuss the two side by side. The peoples of Europe and America have warred and struggled for little else besides liberty these past two or three hundred years and, as a result, democracy is beginning to flourish. The watchword of the French Revolution was "Liberty, Equality, Fraternity," just as the watchword of our Revolution is *"Min-ts'u, Min-ch'uan, Min-sheng"* (People's Nationalism, People's Sovereignty, People's Livelihood). We may say that liberty, equality, and fraternity are based upon the people's sovereignty or that the people's sovereignty develops out of liberty, equality, and fraternity. While we are discussing democracy we must consider the meaning of the French watchword.

As revolutionary ideas have spread through the East, the word "liberty" has come too; many devoted students and supporters of the new movement have sought to explain in detail its meaning, as something of vital importance. The movement for liberty has played a large part in the history of Europe the past two or three hundred years, and most European wars have been fought for liberty. So Western scholars look upon liberty as a most significant thing, and many peoples in the West have engaged in a rewarding study of its meaning. But since the word has been brought to China, only a few of the intelligentsia have had time to study and to understand it. If we should talk to the common people of China in the villages or on the streets about "liberty," they would have no idea of what we meant. So we may say that the Chinese have not gotten anything yet out of the word: even the new youth and the returned students, those who have paid some attention to Western political affairs and those who have constantly heard "liberty" talked about or have seen the word in books, have a very hazy conception of what it signifies. No wonder that foreigners criticize the Chinese, saying that their civilization is inferior and their thinking immature, that they even have no idea of liberty and no word with which to express the idea, yet at the same time criticizing the Chinese for being disunited as a sheet of loose sand.

These two criticisms are absolutely contradictory. What do foreigners mean when they say that China is a sheet of loose sand? Simply that every person does as he pleases and has let his individual liberty extend to all phases of life, hence China is but a lot of separate sand particles. Take up a handful of sand; no matter how much there is, the particles will slip about without any tendency to cohere—that is loose sand. But if we add cement to the loose sand, it will harden into a firm body like a rock, in which the sand, however, has no freedom. When we compare sand and rock, we clearly see that rock was originally composed of particles of sand; but in the firm body of the rock the sand has lost its power to move about freely. Liberty, to put it simply, means the freedom to move about as one wishes within an organized group. Because China dose not have a word to convey this idea, everyone has been at a loss to appreciate it. We have a phrase that suggests liberty—"running wild without bridle," but that is the same thing as "loose sand"—excessive liberty for the individual. So foreigners who criticize us, who say on the one hand that we have no power to unite, are loose sand and free particles, and say on the other hand that we do not understand the meaning of "liberty"—do they not realize that it is everybody's liberty which is making us a sheet of loose sand and that if all are united in a strong body, we cannot be like loose sand? These critics are "holding their spear against their own shield."

Within the last two or three centuries,

foreign countries have expended enormous energy in the struggle for liberty. Is liberty really a good thing? What is it? I don't think the common people of China have the least conception of what this "liberty," that the Westerners say they have been fighting for, means. In their wars, Westerners extolled liberty to the skies and made it sacred; they even made a saying like "Give me liberty or give me death" their battle cry. Chinese students, in translating Western theories, have introduced these words into China; they have upheld liberty and determined to fight for it. In their first enthusiasm they almost equaled the Westerners in days past. But the mass of the people in China do not understand what liberty means; you must realize that liberty develops as the power of the people develops. So in speaking about democracy to-day, I cannot but first speak of liberty. We must understand that Europe and America have shed much blood and have spent mush life in the struggle for liberty. Democracy has been in existence for over a century in the West, but, historically, it followed the fight for liberty. Life was first poured out in order to attain liberty; the fruit of liberty was democracy. In those days the educated leaders of Europe and America held up liberty as their banner just as we in our revolution are holding up the Three Principles of the People. From all this we can see that the Western wars were first for liberty and when liberty was attained the results were called by scholars democracy. The term "democracy" comes from an old Greek word. Even now Westerners are not very much interested in the term "democracy" and think of it more or less as a technical term in political science; it is far from being the matter of life and death which liberty has been.

But in the modern wars of Europe, liberty rather than democracy has been the aim proclaimed. Liberty was a word that everybody in Europe could easily understand. The Europeans' response to the word "liberty" is similar to the Chinese response to-day to the word "make a fortune" which is thought so much of in China. Liberty has been the rallying cry in modern European wars beacuse Europeans understood the word and were willing to contend for it and to sacrifice for it; eyeryone worshiped liberty. Why have Europeans so cherished this word?

The peoples of the West sought liberty because of the extremes to which autocracy had developed. They were in a stage of civilization corresponding to the close of the Chou dynasty and period of the coordinated states in China, about the time of the Roman Empire. Contemporaneously with the Chou, Ch'in, and Han dynasties, Rome was unifying Europe. Rome at first established a republic, but later became a monarchy. After the downfall of the Roman Empire several states sprang up simultaneously in Europe, just as the break-up of the Chou dynasty was followed by the coordinated states. So many scholars have compared the conflict of the "Seven Leaders" at the end of the Chou dynasty with the situation after the fall of Rome. After the Roman Empire had broken up into small states, the feudal system came into existence: the strongest leaders became kings and princes; the next in power, marquises; the least powerful, earls, viscounts, and barons. They all held autocratic power and the whole system of government was far more despotic than the feudal regime during the Chou dynasty in China. We to-day cannot imagine what the people of Europe suffered under their feudal rule; it was far worse than anything Chinese have ever suffered under their autocracies. The reason is this: the Ch'in dynasty* in imposing its autocracy directly on the people would make a human sacrifice of any who spoke evil of government and execute two people for even talking together; soon afterwards the dynasty rushed headlong into ruin. So the dynasties and governments which followed the Ch'in adopted a much more liberal policy towards the people; apart from paying the regular grain taxes the

* 246-207 B. C.

people had almost no relation with the officials. The European tyranny in one way and another pressed directly down upon the shoulders of the common people. As this lasted very long and despotism developed more and more systematically, conditions became worse than anything we have ever experienced in China. So Europeans two hundred years ago were groaning under the painful yoke of autocracy just as Chinese to-day are groaning under the yoke of poverty. Europeans, after such a long period of cruel tyranny, felt keenly the distress which the lack of liberty brought; the only way for them to get rid of their misery was, therefore, to fight for liberty, and when men spoke of liberty, they joyfully responded.

After the destruction of China's ancient feudal system, the stately pomp of autocracy hardly affected the common people. Since the Ch'in dynasty, the aim of China's emperors has been first to protect their own throne that they might continue to keep the empire in their own family and that their heirs might reign in peace forever. So any activities of the people which seemed to endanger the throne were repressed as strongly as possible. So ever since the Ch'in dynasty, succeeding emperors have cared only for their own royal power and but little about the lives of the people. As for the happiness of the people, that was not in their thoughts at all. The people had little direct relation to the emperor beyond paying him the annual grain tax—nothing more. Consequently, the political consciousness of the people has been very weak. The people did not care who was emperor. As soon as they had paid their grain tax they considered their duty as citizens done. The emperors wanted only the grain tax from the people and were not interested in anything else they did, letting them live and die to themselves. We can see from this that the Chinese people have not been directly subject to the oppression of autocracy; their sufferings have come indirectly. Because our state has been weak, we have come under the political and economic domination of foreign countries and have not been able to resist. Now our wealth is exhausted and our people are destitute, suffering poverty because of an indirect tyranny.

The Chinese people, therefore, felt very little resentment against their emperors. On the other hand, the autocracy of Europe was quite different from that of China. The despotism in Europe, from the downfall of Rome up to two or three centuries ago, had been developing rapidly and the people had suffered increasingly and unbearably. Many kinds of liberty were denied them, chiefly liberty of thought, liberty of speech, and liberty of movement. Take freedom of belief. When people who live in a certain place are forced to believe in a particular religion, whether they want to or not, the situation becomes very hard to bear. Europeans indeed suffered "deep waters and burning fires" from the denial of freedom. So, whenever they heard of anyone leading a struggle for liberty, they all rejoiced and espoused his cause. Such was the beginning of the European revolutionary idea.

There is a deep significance in the proposal of our Revolutionary Party that the Three Principles of the People, rather than a struggle for liberty, should be the basis of our revolution. The watchword of the French Revolution was "Liberty"; the watchword of the American Revolution was "Independence"; the watchword of our Revolution is the "Three Principles of the People." We spent much time and effort before we decided upon our watchword; we are not merely imitating others. The peoples of Europe suffered so bitterly from despotism that as soon as the banner of liberty was lifted high, millions with one heart rallied about it. If we in China, where the people have not suffered such despotism, should make the cry of liberty, no attention would be paid to it.

Modern European scholars who observe China all say that our civilization is so backward and our political consciousness so weak that we do not even understand liberty. "We Europeans," they declare, "fought and sacrificed for liberty one or two hundred years ago and performed no one knows how many startling deeds, but Chinese still do not know what liberty is. This shows that the political thinking of us Europeans is far superior to the political thinking of the Chinese." Because we do not talk about liberty, they say that we are poor in political ideas. I don't think such an argument gets anywhere. If Europeans value liberty so much, why do they call the Chinese a "sheet of loose sand"? When Europeans were struggling for liberty, they naturally took a strong view of liberty, but since they have won liberty and have reached their goal, their conception of liberty has probably become weaker. If the banner of liberty should be raised again to-day, I don't think it would call forth the same enthusiasm as before. Moreover, struggles for liberty was the European method of revolution two or three centuries ago and could not be repeated now. To use the figure "loose sand," what is its chief characteristic?—Its absolute freedom, without which there can be no such thing as loose sand. When European democracy was just budding, Europeans talked aboutt fighting for liberty; when they had gained their end, everyone began to extend the limits of his individual liberty and soon the excesses of liberty led to many evil consequences. Therefore an English scholar named Mill* said that only individual liberty which did interfere with the liberty of others can be considered true liberty. If one's liberty is incompatible with another's sphere of liberty, it is no longer liberty. Before that, Westerners had set no limits upon freedom, but when Mill proposed his theory of a limited freedom, the measure of personal liberty was considerably reduced. Evidently Western scholars had come to realize that liberty was not a sacred thing which could not be encroached upon, but that it must be put within boundaries.

* Referring to John Stuart Mill.

When we think about that "sheet of loose sand",we realize that the Chinese have had a great measure of liberty. Because Chinese have had an excessive degree of liberty, they have given it no concern, just as when there is plenty of fresh air in the room, we do not realize its value; but when the doors and the windows are closed and no fresh air can come in, we know its importance. Europeans under the despotism of two or three centuries ago had no liberty whatsoever, so every man appreciated how precious a thing liberty was and was ready to give his life for it. Before they won liberty, they were like men shut up in a small room; after they had won liberty they were like men suddenly let out into the open air. Naturally everyone felt that liberty was something of wonderful value and was saying, "Give me liberty or give me death."

Europeans and Americans risked their lives in the battles for liberty a hundred and fifty years ago, because liberty was rare for them. When nations like France and the United States won liberty, they became what we call the pioneers in democratic government. Yet even in these two countries, is evryone free? The liberty which Westerners talk about has its strict limitations and cannot be described as belonging to everyone. Young Chinese students when they talk about liberty break down all restraints. Because no one welcomes their theory in the scoiety outside, they can only bring it back into their own schools, and con-stant disorders and strikes result. This is abuse of freedom. That foreigners should not be familiar with Chinese history and should not know that since ancient times Chinese have enjoyed a large measure of liberty, is not strange. But that our own students should have forgotten the Liberty Song of the ancient Chinese—

"When the sun rises, I toil;
When the sun sets, I rest;
I dig wells for water;
I till the fields for food;
What has the Emperor's power to do with

me?"

is surprisingly strange. We can see from this Liberty Song that China, while she has not had liberty in name, has had liberty in fact from days of old, and so much of it that she need not seek for more.

If foreigners say that we are a sheet of loose sand, we will acknowledge the truth, but we cannot accept their assertion that the Chinese have no understanding of liberty and are weak in their political consciousness. Why has China become a sheet of loose sand? Simply because of excessive individual liberty. Therefore the aims of the Chinese Revolution are different from the aims in foreign revolutions, and the methods we use must also be different. Why, indeed, is China having a revolution? To put the answer directly, the aims of our revolution are just opposite to the aims of the revolutions of Europe. Europeans rebelled and fought for liberty because they had had too little liberty. But we, because we have had too much liberty without any unity and resisting power, because we have become a sheet of loose sand and so have been invaded by foreign imperialism and oppressed by the economic control and trade wars of the Powers, without being able to resist, must break down individual liberty and become pressed together into an unyielding body like the firm rock which is formed by the addition of cement to sand.

Western revolutions began with the struggle for liberty; only after war and agitation of two or three centuries was the liberty realized from which democracy sprang. The watchword of the French Revolution was "Liberty, Equality, Fraternity." Our watchword is "People's Nationalism, People's Sovereignty, People's Livelihood." What relation do the two watchwords have to each other? According to my interpretation, our Nationalism may be said to correspond to their Liberty, because putting the People's Nationalism into effect means a struggle for the liberty of our nation. The Europeans fought for individual liberty, but to-day we have a different use for liberty. Now how shall the term "liberty" be applied? If we apply it to a person, we shall become a sheet of loose sand; on no account must we give more liberty to the individual; let us secure liberty instead for the nation. The individual should not have too much liberty, but the nation should have complete liberty. When the nation can act freely, then China may be called strong. To make the nation free, we each sacrifice his personal freedom. Students who sacrifice their personal liberty will be able to work diligently day after day and spend time and effort upon learning; when their studies are completed, their knowledge is enlarged and their powers have multiplied, then they can do things for the nation. Soldiers who sacrifice their personal liberty will be able to obey orders, repay their country with loyalty and help the nation to attain liberty. If students and soldiers talk liberty, they will soon have "unrestrained license," to use a Chinese phrase for liberty. Schools will have no rules and the army will have no discipline. How can you have a school without rules? What kind of army is that without disipline?

Why do we want the nation to be free? — Because China under the domination of the Powers has lost her national standing. She is not merely a semi-colony; she has indeed become a hypo-colony. If we want to restore China's liberty, we must unite ourselves into one unshakable body; we must use revolutionary methods to weld our state into firm unity. Without revolutionary principles we shall never succeed. Our revolutionary principles are the cement. If we can consolidate our four hundred millions and form a mighty union and make the union free, the Chinese state will be free and the Chinese people will be really free. Compare the watchword of the French Revolution with that of ours. "Liberty" in the French revolutionary watchword and "People's Nationalism" in our watchword are similar. The People's Nationalism calls for the freedom of our nation. "Equality" is similar to our "Principle of the People's Sovereignty" which aims to destroy autocracy and make all men equal. "Fraternity" originally meant brothers and has the same significance as the Chinese word *t'ung-pao* (compatriots). The idea in "Fraternity" is similar to our "Principle of the People's Livelihood," which plans for the happiness of our four hundred millions.

LECTURE THREE

Min-ch'uan, the People's Sovereignty, is the second part of our revolutionary watchword and corresponds to equality in the French watchword. So to-day let us take equality as the theme for our study. The word "equality" is usually associated with the word "liberty." During the former revolutions in the various countries of Europe, all the people expended an almost equal amount of strength and sacrified to a similar degree in their fight for liberty and equality, and consequently they valued equality as much as they did liberty. Moreover, many people felt that if they could secure liberty, they would certainly attain to equality, and that if they did not become equal, there was no manifest their freedom; they regarded equality as being even higher than liberty. What is equality and whence does it come? The revolutionary philosophy of Europe and America spoke of liberty as something bestowed by Nature upon man. For example, the "Declaration of Independence" of the American Revolution and the "Declaration of the Rights of Man and of the Citizen" of the French Revolution both pronouncedly and emphatically proclaimed that liberty and equality were natural and inalienable rights of man.

Are men really born with the special right of equality? We traced the history of people's rights from the age of primitive man millions of years ago down to the beginning of our modern democratic period, but we did not discover any principle of natural human equality. In the world of Nature we do not find any two things level, except upon the surface of water. On level ground there is no place truly level. The railway runs through a natural plane; but if you look out of your coach window along the way and observe carefully the contour of the land, you will find that there is not a mile of track but has required human labor engineering to make it level.

Nature originally did not make man equal; but when autocracy developed among mankind, the despotic kings and princes pushed human differences to an extreme, and the result was an inequality far worse than Nature's inequality. The inequality created by kings and princes was an artificial inequality. To illustrate the conditions it resulted in, let me draw a diagram on the blackboard here:

DIAGRAM I—INEQUALITY

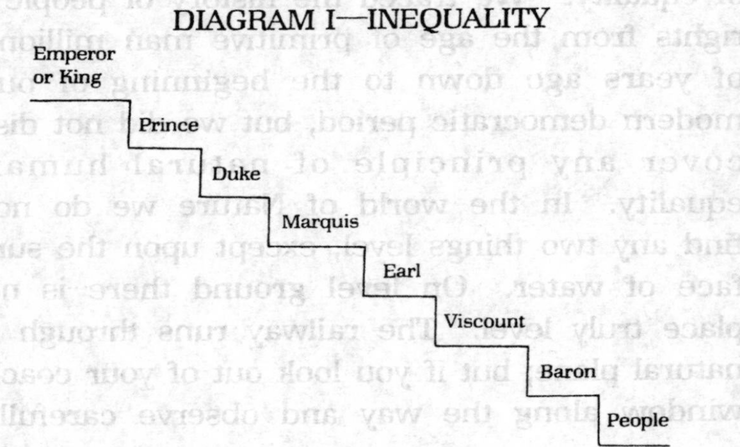

Study this diagram carefully and you will understand what artificial inequality meant. Because of these artificial ranks, the specially privileged classes became excessively cruel and iniquitous, while the oppressed people, unable to contain themselves, finally broke into rebellion and warred upon inequality. The original aim in the revolutions had been the destruction of man-made inequalities; when that was completed, men thought their revolution would be over. But the men who occupied the high stations of emperor and king all assumed a divine appointment as a shield for their office; they said that they had received their special position from God and that the people who opposed them would be opposing God. The ignorant masses, who did not study to see whether there were any truth or not in these words, followed on blindly and fought for more privileges for their kings. They even opposed the intelligent people who talked about equality and liberty. So the scholars who were supporting revolution had to invent the theory of nature-bestowed rights of equality and liberty in order to overthrow the despotism of kings. Their orginal purpose was to break down artificial, man-made inequalities. But in everything, certainly, "action is easy, understanding difficult"; the masses of Europe at that time believed that emperors and kings were divinely sent and had special "divine rights," and large numbers of ignorant folk supported them. No matter what methods or how much energy the small group of intelligent and educated people used, they could not overthrow the monarchs.

Finally, when the belief that man is born free and equal and that the struggle for freedom and equality is the duty of everybody had permeated the masses, the emperors and kings of Europe fell automatically. But after their downfall, the people began to believe firmly in the theory of natural equality and kept on working day after day to make all men equal. They did not know that such a thing is impossible. Only recently, in the light of science, have people begun to realize that there is no principle of natural equality. If we acted according to the belief of the masses at that time, regardless of the truth, and forced an equality upon human society, that equality would be a false one.

DIAGRAM II—FALSE EQUALITY

The Sage
The Superior Man
THe Genius
The Wise Man
The Average Man
The Mediocre Man
The Dullard
The Inferior Man

As this second diagram shows, we would have to level down superior position in order to get equality at the top, but the line representing the standing ground of these different type would still be uneven and not level. The equality we secured would be a false equality. Equal position in human society is something to start with; each man builds up his career upon this start according to his natural endowments of intelligence and ability. As each man has different gifts of intelligence andability, so the resultant careers will be different. And since each man works differently, they certainly cannot work on an equal basis. This brings us to only true principle of equality. If we pay no attention to each man's intellectual endowments and capacities and push down those who rise to a high position in order to make all equal, the world will not progress and mankind will retrocede. When we speak of democracy and equality but yet want the world to advance, we are talking about political equality. For equality is an artificial not a natural thing, and the only equality which we can create is equality in political status.

DIAGRAM III—TRUE EQUALITY

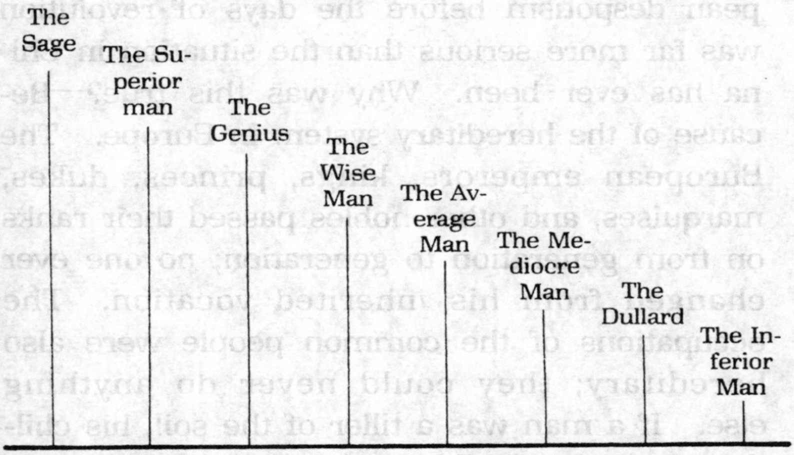

The Sage
The Superior man
The Genius
The Wise Man
The Average Man
The Mediocre Man
The Dullard
The Inferior Man

After the revolution, we want every man to have an equality political standing, such as is represented by the base line in Diagram III

This is the only true equality and true principle of nature.

The situation which existed under European despotism before the days of revolution was far more serious than the situation in China has ever been. Why was this true?—Because of the hereditary system in Europe. The European emperors, kings, princes, dukes, marquises, and other nobles passed their ranks on from generation to generation; no one ever changed from his inherited vocation. The occupations of the common people were also hereditary; they could never do anything else. If a man was a tiller of the soil, his children and grandchildren would be farmers. A laborer's children and grandchildren would have to do bitter toil. The grandson could not choose a different occupation from his grandfather's. This inability to change one's profession was the kind of inequality which existed at that time in Europe. Since the breakup of the feudal system in China, these professional barriers have also been entirely destroyed. Thus we see that while China along with foreign countries has had a class system and kind of inequality, yet China has had the advantage, since only the emperor's rank was hereditary. Unless the emperor was overthrown, the right to reign was passed from one generation to another in the same family. Only when there was a change of dynasty did the line of emperors change. But as for dukes, marquises, earls, viscounts, and barons, these titles were changed from one generation to another even in olden day. Many commoners have become ministers of state or have been appointed princes and nobles; these were not hereditary offices. There may have been a few commoners in Europe who became ministers to state or were elevated to the nobility, but the majority of titles were hereditary and the common people were not free in choosing their occupations. This lack of freedom was what caused them to lose their equality. Not only were the political ranks not equal, but the social classes of the common people were unequal. Consequently, it was very diffcult for the common people, first, to reach the position of duke, marquis, earl, viscount, or baron, and, second, to change their own occupations freely and thus rise in life. At last they came to feel that they could no longer endure the afflictions of this system, that they must throw their lives into a struggle for liberty, emancipate themselves from non—freedom of occupation and strive to progress. Such a war for liberty, such a demolishing of tyannical class inequality, has never been witnessed in China. Although the Chinese have experienced class distinctions, yet they have never sacrificed their own lives or their families as a price for liberty. The revolutions of the European peoples have concentrated upon achieving liberty and equality, but the Chinese have never really understood what these things mean. The reason for this is that China's autocracy, in comparison with Europe's has not been at all severe. And although China's government was autocratic in ancient times and has not made any progress in the last two thousand years, yet before that period many reforms had been made and the abuse of despotism had been considerably reduced. Consequently, the people have not suffered very much from the autocratic system and have not fought for the principle of equality.

Since European civilization has spread its influence eastward, European political systems, economics, and science have also penetrated China. When the Chinese hear European political doctrines they generally copy them word for word without any thought of modification. The European revolutions two and three centuries ago were "struggles for liberty," so China now must struggle for liberty! Europeans fought for equality, so China must fight for equality also! But China's weakness to-day is not the lack of liberty and equality. If we try to arouse the spirit of the people with "Liberty and Equality," we will be talking wide of the point. Our people are not out deeply enough by these things; they are not sensitive to them, and so would certainly not join our banner. But the people of Europe two or three centuries ago suffered "waters of tribulation and fires of torment" from the loss of liberty and equality; they felt that unless they could achieve liberty and equality, no question could be solved, and so they hazarded their lives in the struggle for them.

Take the United States again. The objective in the minds of the American people during their revolution was independence. Why? Because their thirteen colonies were all British territory and under British control. Great Britain was a despotic monarchy and was oppressing the American people much more severely than she oppressed her own people. When the Americans saw that they and the British were under the same government, but that British citizens were treated liberally while they themselves were so much abused, they felt keenly the inequality in the situation; they wanted to secede from Britain, govern themselves, and establish an independent state. For the sake of independence they resisted Britain and engaged in war with her for eight years until they achieved their purpose. The American government has treated its white races alike, on a basis of equality, but its treatment of colored races has been very different. The African negroes, for instance, were looked upon as slaves. Then there were many earnest people who made investigations into the sufferings of the negro slaves and published reports of what they saw. The most famous of these described many actual tragic facts of slave life in the form of a novel, which was read by everybody with intense interest. This book was called "The Black Slave's Cry to Heaven"* and when it came out, people realized what the slaves were enduring and were indignant on their behalf. Then all

* Chinese title of Uncle Tom's Cabin.

the Northern States which did not use slave labor advocated the freeing of the slaves. The Southern States owned a vast number of slaves; each southern state had numerous vast plantations which depended solely upon slave labor for cutivation. If they should free the slaves, they would have no hard labor and could not plant their fields. The Southerners, from selfish motives, opposed emancipation, saying that the slave system was not started by one man only.

Therefore, although agitation for the freeing of the slaves had begun long before, there was still a period of ferment, and it is only sixty years since the final explosion took place, precipitating the war between the North and the South. This war lasted five years, and was one of the world's great wars. It was a war against the inequality of the black slave, a war against human inequality, a war for equality.

The war resulted in defeat for the South and victory for the North, and the government of the United States immedately issued a proclamation freeing the slaves throughout the country.

The freeing of the slaves was one of the struggles for equality in American history. The two finest periods in American history were: first, when the people, suffering under the unequal treatment of the British, waged the War of Independence and, after eight years of fighting, broke away from Britain and established an independent state; second, when sixty years later the war between the North and the South was fought, for a cause similar to that of the War for Independence. The Civil War lasted five years, while the Revolutionary War lasted eight years. So American history is a story of struggle for equality and makes a shining page in the history of the world.

After the war for equality in America, a revolutionary struggle for equality broke out in France also. The conflict experienced vicissitudes over a period of eighty years before it could be counted a success. But after equality had been secured, the people pushed the word "equality" to an extreme and wanted to put everyone on the same level. It was the kind of equality which diagram Ⅱ represents: the line of equality was not placed underfoot but overhead—false equality.

China's tide of revolutionary ideas came from Europe and American, and the theory of equality has also been introduced from the West. But our Revolutionary Party advocates a struggle, not for liberty and equality, but for the Three Principles of the People. If we can put these Three Principles into practice, we will have liberty and equality. Although Western nations warred for liberty and equality, they have since been constantly led astray by them. If we put the Three Principles into operation and achieve true liberty and equality, how can we be sure to keep on the right track? If, as in Diagram Ⅱ, we put the line of equality at the top, we will not be following the right course. But if, as in Diagram Ⅲ, we make the line of equality the base upon which to stand, we will be on the right track of equality. So if we want to know whether the principles we are using in our revolution are desirable or not and whether they are following the right line, we must first study carefully the history of European revolutions from their very beginnings. And if people want to understand thoroughly our Three Principles and to know whether they are really a good thing, suitable to the needs of our country, if they want to be able to believe in our Three Principles and never waver in their faith, they, too, must study carefully the history of Western revolutions from their inception.

Without democracy, liberty and equality would have been but empty terms. The origin of democracy lies far back in history; two thousand or more years ago Rome and Greece already had ideas of people's rights and were democratic states. South of the Mediterranean, at the same time was another republic called Carthage, and several small states which sprang up in succession afterwards were also republics. Although Rome and Greece of that day were democracies in name, in reality they had not attained to true liberty and equality. The people's sovereignty had not been applied. Greece had the slaves system; the nobility all owned many slaves; in fact, two thirds of all the populatiion were slaves. The warriors of Sparta were each given five slave attendants by the state. So in Greece the people with sovereign rights were a small minority; the large majority had no rights. The same thing was true in Rome. So Greece and Rome two thousand years ago were republics only in name; still having their slave system, they could not realize the ideal of liberty and equality. Not until the United States, sixty years ago, freed her slaves, smashed the slave system, and made the equality of mankind a reality did the hope of true liberty and equality begin to appear in modern democracy. True liberty and equality stand upon democracy and are dependent upon democracy. Only where democracy flourishes can liberty and equality permanently survive; there is no way to preserve them if the sovereignty of the people is lost. So the Revolutionary Party of China, in its inception took liberty and equality as aims in its struggle but made Democracy—the Sovereignty of People—its principle and watchword. Only if we achieve democracy can our people have the reality and enjoy the blessings of freedom and liberty. They are embraced in our principle of the People's Sovereignty, hence we are discussing them in connection with our main theme.

After struggling so hard and pouring out so much blood for liberty and equality, how highly should we expect Europe and America to value these principles! How careful they should be to weigh them and not recklessly to abuse them! But the truth is, as I have said before, that many evil practices have flowed from the newly acquired liberty of the West. It is more than one hundered years since the American and French revolutions secured equality. Has equality, too, been abused? I think it has. We cannot afford, after the experience of Western nations, to follow in their tracks and fight only for equality. We must fight for democracy; if democracy prevails, we shall have true equality; if democacy languishes, we can never have equality.

In our revolution we must not talk only about getting equality; we must hold up the people's rights. Unless democracy is fully developed, the equality which we fight for will be only temporary and will soon disappear. But although our revolution does not make Equality its slogan, still we do include equality in the Sovereignty of the People. When equality is a good thing we will apply it; when it is an evil, we will do away with it. Only thus can we make democracy develop and use equality to advantage.

I once suggested that the people of the world might be divided, according to their natural endowments, into three groups: those who know and perceive beforehand, those who know and perceive afterward, and those who do not know and perceive—the discoverers, the promoters, and the practical men. If these three groups could use each other and heartily cooperate, human civilization would advance "a thousand miles a day."

Although Nature produces men with varying intelligence and ability, yet the human heart has continued to hope that all men might be equal. This is the highest of moral ideals and mankind should earnestly strive towards it. But how shall we begin? We will better understand by contrasting two philosophies of life—the selfish which benefits self and the altruistic which benefits other. Those who are out for themselves are continually injuring others with no pang of conscience. When this philosophy prevailed, intelligent and able men used all their powers to seize others' rights and privileges, gradually formed an autocratic caste, and created political inequalities—that was the world before the revolutions for democracy. Those who are concerned with benefiting others are glad to sacrifice themselves. Where this philosophy prevails, intelligent and able men are ever ready to use all their powers for the welfare of others, and religions of love and philanthropic enterprises grow up. But religious power alone is insufficient and philanthropy alone cannot remedy all evil. So we must seek a fundamental solution, effect a revolution, overthrow autocracy, life up democracy, and level inequalities. Hereafter we should harmonize the three types which I have described and give them all equal standing. Everyone should make service, not exploitation, his aim. Those with greater intelligence and ability should serve thousands and ten thousands to the limit of their power and make thousands and ten thousands happy. Those with less intelligence and ability thould serve tens and hundreds to the limit of their power and make tens and hundreds happy. The saying, "The skillful the slaves of the stupid" is just this principle. Those who have neither intelligence nor ability should still, to the limit of their individual power, each serve one another and make one another happy. In this way, although men now may vary in natural intelligence and ability, yet as moral ideals and the spirit of service prevail, they will certainly become more and more equal. This is the essence of equality.

LECTURE FOUR

Delivered on April 13, 1924.

In the preceding lectures we saw that Europeans and Americans have been engaged for two or three centuries in their struggle for democracy. To-day I want to speak about the measure of people's rights which they have won the progress which they have made in democracy during this period. Look at the so-called pioneers of democratic government in the West, like the United States and France, whose revolutions took place over a century ago—how many political rights have the people really won? To the believer in democracy, it seems that the people have gained but very little power. Those who fought for the people's rights thought that they would reach the democratic ideal at once, so they sacrificed everything and pooled all their resources of strength in a life and death struggle. But after they had conquered in battle, they found that they had gained much less power than they had hoped for during the revolution. They had not yet attained to perfect democracy.

Take once more the American War of Independence against Great Britain. It took eight years for colonies to win the war and to achieve their ideals of popular sovereignty. According to the Declaration of Independence, liberty and equality are natural and inalienable rights. The American revolutionists had hoped to win complete freedom and equality, yet after their eight years of struggle they still did not enjoy many popular rights. Why? The great enemy to the people's sovereignty in the American colonies was the British king; his oppressions gave rise to a war of democracy against autocracy. Since the war resulted in victory for democrary, it seems that people should have gained all their rights. But why was the democratic ideal not realized? Because, after independence had been won and autocracy had been overthrown, problems as to the administration of democratic government arose among its supporters. How far could popular sovereignty be actually applied? Here the fellow disciples of democracy began to differ in their opinions. As a result there was a division into two great parties. You have all heard of the illustrious leader of the American Revolution, the father-statesman of the United States—Washington. But there were other heroes also who helped him in his struggle against Great Britain. Among these were Washington's secretary of the treasury, Hamilton, and his secretary of state, Jefferson. As these two men differed radically over methods of administration and as both had large followings, they became the founders of two absolutely different political parties. Jefferson's party believed that the people were endowed with natual rights and that if the people were given complete democratic power, they would be discriminating in the use of their freedom, would direct their power to the accomplishment of great tasks, and would make all the affairs of the nation progress to the fullest extent. Jefferson's theory assumed that human nature is naturally good, and that if the people under complete democratic rule sometimes do not express their natural virtue and do good but abuse their power and do evil, it is because they have met some obstacle and are for the time being forced to act that way. In short, every man is naturally endowed with freedom and equality and hence should have political power; every man is intelligent and if given political power to govern would do great things for the nation; if all the citizens would shoulder the responsibility for good government, the state would prosper long in peace. Such was the Jeffersonian party's faith in the rights of the people.

The policy proposed by Hamilton's party was directly opposed Jefferson's ideas. Hamilton did not think that human nature was always perfect; and he felt that, if democratic power were given equally to all men, bad men would direct their political power to bad ends. And if corrupt individuals should get much of the power of the state into their hands, they would use the rights and privileges of the state for the selfish benefit and profit of their own party; they would not care a rap for any morality, law, justice, or order in the nation, and the final result would be either a "state with three rulers"—divided authority and want of unity—or mob rule, that is, liberty and equality pushed to excess and anarchy. Such an application of democracy would not advance the nation but would only throw it into disorder and make it lose ground. So Hamilton proposed that the political power of the state should not be given entirely to the people, but should be centralized in the government, in a central authority; the common people should have only a limited degree of democracy. If the people should all have unlimited power and should use it for evil, the effect upon the nation would be far more serious than the evil deeds of one king. A wicked king still has many people to oversee him and restrain him, but a people who get unlimited power into their hands and use it for wicked purposes have none to oversee and restrain them. Therefore Hamilton declared that, as autocracy had to be restricted, so democracy must also be limited, and he founded the Federalist Party which advocated the centralization and not the diffusion of sovereign power.

Before the War of Independence the thirteen original colonies were governed by Great Britain and were unable to unite. Later, when they found that they could not endure the extreme despotism of the British government, they resisted, and out of their common aim a common spirit was born. But after the war, the colonies again divided and found themselves unable to agree.

After the states had secured their independence, they were no longer troubled by enemies within, but their three million people were scattered throughout thirteen states with not over two hundred thousand in any one state, and the states did not get along well together. Since they would not unite, the nation's power was weak; it might easily be swallowed up by another European power. The future was full of dangers. Then the farseeing statesmen of the different states saw that they must increase their national strength tremendously if they wanted to avert the dangers ahead and establish a permanent nation. So they proposed that all the states unite and form one great state. Some advocated purely popular sovereignty and others purely national sovereignty as a means of bringing about union. The former group advocated local authority, the latter group advocated centralized authority and the limitation of the people's power. They wanted the states all to pool their own rights and powers in a strong central government, and so were called the Federalists. The fight waged between these two opposing groups by mouth and pen war long and bitter. Finally the Federalists who advocated the limitation of popular sovereignty won out, the states got together, formed a federal union, and promulgated the Constitution of the United States. From the beginning of the Republic until now the United States has used this Constitution, which divides clearly the legislative, judicial, and executive powers of the government so that they do not encroach upon each other. It was the first complete constitution in human history and the United States was the first nation to adopt a written constitution separating the three branches of government. This constitution is what we call the Federal Constitution of the United States. Since the United States formed a federal union and adapted the Constitution, it has become the wealthiest and, since the European War, the most powerful nation in the world.

Because the United States started on the road to its present position of wealth and power from a federal constitution which yet leaves the local affairs of the people to state control, a group of Chinese intellectuals and scholars during the last decade have been proposing that China, in order to be wealthy and strong, must also form a federal union. They have thought to solve China's present problems, but they have not made a fundamental comparison of the conditions in the United States and in China; their only argument is that since a federal union made the United States wealthy and strong, and since China's great hope is to be wealthy and strong, therefore we should have a federal union of the provinces. The fundamental advantage of the American federal system came from the fact that each state already had a constitution and a government of its own. If we want to follow the United States' federal plan and form a union of provinces, all the provinces should first adopt constitutions and establish their own governments, then unite and decide upon a national constitution. In a word, we would have to take our already united China, divide it into twenty-odd independent units to correspond with the dozen or so independent American states over a century ago, and then weld them together again. Such views and ideas are utterly fallacious. We become mere parrots, repeating with our eyes shut what others tell us. Because the United States, with its federal system, has become the world's wealthiest and greatest power, we think that we must copy her system in order that China may be wealthy and strong. This is similar to what I have said before: while Westerners fought for democracy, they did not talk about democracy but about liberty and equality; so we Chinese in our revolution must take the Western slogans and cry that we are struggling for liberty and equality! All this is but blind following and foolish incomprehension. We see that the provinces in past history have been united, not separate, parts of China and have not been incapable of unified rule. Moreover, the periods of unity have been the periods of good government; the periods of disunity, the periods of disorder. The United States' wealth and power have not come only from the independence and self-government of the original states, but rather from the progress in unified government which followed the federation of the states. Her wealth and power were the result of the union of the states, not of the division into states. Since China was originally unified we should not divide her again into separate provinces. If we say that the American federal system is the key to wealth and power, we are putting effect before cause.

When the thirteen American states secured their independence from England, they had absolutely no political unity, and the formation of a unified nation was a tremendously difficult task. So the debates between the parties of Hamilton and Jefferson were very fierce. When the Constitution was drawn up, each state was given freedom in casting votes. Finally, Hamilton's party won out and the Jeffersonian policy began to lose ground. Because the people of the country at the time when the Constitution was framed were divided into these two great parties with different political theories, the Constitution which was finally promulgated was a document of compromise between the two parties. The important political powers which belonged to the central government were clearly defined in the Constitution, matters not regulated by the Constitution were left to local governments. The coinage of money, for example, was put under control of the central government, and local governments were not allowed to transgress upon this right. Foreign relations were delegated to the central government and no state could make a private treaty with a foreign country. Other matters, like national defense, the training of troops upon land and sea, the right to move and dispatch state militia, were all intrusted to the central government. Matters of detail which were not delegated by the Constitution to the central government were left to the individual states to regulate. This division of power was a compromise measure between the central government and the state governments. What rights did the people obtain out of this compromise? —Only a limited suffrage. The suffrage at that time was limited to the election of congressmen and of various state and local officials. The president and the senators were still elected indirectly by electors chosen by the people. Later the powers of the people were gradually enlarged until to-day the president, the senators, and all state and local officials who have any direct, important relation with the people are elected by direct popular vote. This is what we call universal suffrage.

Therefore, the evolution in the United States from limited to universal suffrage was very gradual. At first suffrage was enjoyed only by men. Only a decade or two ago women still did not have the right to vote. Twenty years ago the movement for woman suffrage became very strong in Europe and America. You all know that at that time many people felt that the women would not succeed in their struggle on the ground that they were inferior in intellect and ability to men and could not do all the things that men could do. So there were many opponents of woman suffrage not only among men but even among the women themselves. Even if all the women of the nation had fought violently for the right to vote, they could hardly have hoped to succeed. But seven or eight years ago the women of Great Britain, and not long afterwand the women of the United States, were successful in their struggle. The cause was the European War. During the war, the men went into the army and spent their strength upon the battlefields. Çonsequently, much of the nation's business was left without men to care for it; there were not enough men to be officers and day laborers in the arsenals, to be engineers and conductors on the street cars, and to assume responsibility for the various kinds of business which required energetic attention at the home base. Women were called upon to fill men's jobs, and then those who had opposed woman suffrage, saying that women could not do the work of men, were stripped of their arguments and no longer dared to thwart the movement. The advocates of woman suffrage then won a complete victory and after the war the question was finally settled. From this we can see that the objective of the Western revolutions was originally democracy. The American War of Independence was a war for democracy; after the war, however, comrades in the cause divided into two groups—one group advocating complete democracy, the other group advocating limited powers for the people but large powers for the state. Many later events went to prove that the common people did not possess the necessary intelligence and power to wield complete sovereignty. That Jefferson and his disciples tried to obtain more rights for the people, but failed, shows that the common people did not know how to exercise political sovereignty. So, although the Western revolutions of these two or three hundred years have been carried out under the standard of democracy, the actual result has only been the attainment of suffrage for men and women.

The French Revolution also set up democracy as its goal. Scholarly advocates of democracy like Rousseau declared that all men had natural rights which kings and princes could not take away, and such theories gave birth to the revolution. When democracy began to be applied after the revolution, nobles and members of the royal house received so many injuries that they were unable to remain in France and had to flee to other countries. The French people were now making their first experiment in complete democracy; no one in the country dared to say that the people did not have intelligence and power; if one did, he would be accused of being a counter-revolutionist and would immediately be brought to the guillotine. The result was that a mob tyranny was instituted. Anarchy followed, society was panic-stricken, no one was sure of his life from morning till evening. Even a regular member of the revolutionary party might, because of a careless word which offended the multitude, be sentenced to death. In this experiment at pure democracy, not only were many princes, lords, and nobles killed, but not a few ardent revolutionists of the time, like Danton, were put to death by the populace because of some word that did not please them. When the French people afterwards came to realize that such a state of affairs was too oppressive, many who had been eager supporters of democracy grew despondent and cold, turned against democratic government, and supported Napoleon for emperor. Democracy now met a great obstacle. Not from autocracy: the democratic movement had already become powerful and , as I have been saying, the world had reached the age of democracy. It stood to reason that democracy would steadily advance. Why, then, after democracy had overthrown autocracy, did such barriers to the progress of democracy arise? What created them? One cause was the attitude of the conservative supporters of democracy who advocated definite´ limitation of the people's sovereignty and centralization of the state's sower, rather than complete democracy. But this group was not powerful and did not impede the progress of democracy very seriously. The real obstructionists were the believers in absolute democracy. When, during the French Revolution, the people secured complete power, they no longer wanted leaders and they put to death many of the wise and able ones. The groups of violent followers who were left were devoid of clear perception and were easily made tools of by others. Without their " good ears and eyes " the people of the nation were unable to distinguish who was right and who was wrong in any issue that rose; only let someone incite them and everyone would blindly follow. Such a state of affairs was extremely perilous. So when the people awoke to it in the course of time, they did not dare to advocate democracy again. Out of this reaction against democracy developed a great obstacle to the progress of democracy, an obstacle created by the very people who advocated people's rights.

Since the American and the French Revolution, democratic ideals have been spreading steadily throughout the world. The newest theories of democracy owe their real origin, however, to Germany. The German mind has always been rich in democratic ideas; labor unions are numerous in Germany. Democratic philosophy developed early in Germany, but up to the time of the European War it had not produced as much fruit as in France or Great Britain. The reason was that the methods used by the German government in dealing with democracy were different from those used by the British government ; therefore, the results attained were also different. What were the methods used by German government ? Who hindered the growth of democracy in Germany? Many students say that the setback began with Bismarck.

From the establishment of the German Confederation until before the European War,

Germany was the strongest state in the world. She was the master of Europe and the nations of Europe followed her as a leading horse. Germany was raised to her eminent position entirely by the creative arm of Bismarck. Within twenty years after he had taken charge of the government, Bismarck transformed a weak Germany into a powerful state. After such an achievement, democracy while it flourished in Germany did not have sufficient strength to challenge the government.

While Bismarck was in power, he not only dominated the world in political and military affairs and in all kinds of diplomacy, but he also used consummate skill in dealing with the democratic movement and in winning victories over his own people. In the latter part of the nineteenth century, after the Franco-Prussian War, economic wars as well as wars for democracy began to break out. The hot passion for democracy was gradually cooling, but something else was being born—socialism. Socialism is similar to the Principle of the People's Livelihood, which I have been advocating. At that time German socialism had a very wide influence.

Socialism was originally closely related to democracy and the two should have developed simultaneously. But why did democratic ideas in Europe give rise to democratic revolutions, while the spread of socialist theories failed to give rise to economic revolutions?—Because the birth of socialism in Germany coincided with Bismarck's regime. Other men would certainly have used political force to crush socialism, but Bismarck chose to employ other methods. He knew that the German people were enlightened and that the labor organizations were firmly established; if he attempted the suppression of socialism by political force, he would only labor in vain. Bismarck had already been in favor of absolute control by a centralized authority. What menhods did he use to deal with the socialistos? The Socialist Party advocated social reforms and economic revolution. Bismarck knew that they could not be suppressed by political power, so he put into effect a kind of state socialism as an antidote against the Marxian socialists' program. At the time when Bismarck was seizing the reins of government in Germany, most of the railways in Great Britain and France were privately owned. Because the capital industries were owned by the wealthy, all the industries of the nation became monopolies of the wealthy class, and the many evils of an unequal distribution of wealth began to appear. Bismarck did not want such condition in Germany, so he put into effect a state socialism; he brought all the railways of the country under state ownership and control and put all the essential industries under state management. He determined upon hours of labor and arranged for old-age pensions and accident insurance for the workers. These measures were items in the program of reform which the Socialist Party was trying to carry out; the farseeing Bismarck took the lead and used the state's power to accomplish them. Moreover, he used the profits from the state-managed railways, banks, and other businesses for the protection of workers, which of course made the workers very contented. Before this, several hundred thousand workers had been leaving Germany for other countries every year, but after Bismarck's economic policy was put into effect, not only did no more German workers leave but many came from other countries to work in Germany. Bismarck met socialism by anticipating it and by taking precautions against it, rather than by a head-on attack upon it; by invisible means he caused the very issues for which the people were struggling to dissolve. When there was nothing left for the people to fight for, revolutions naturally did not break out. This was the artful method by which Bismarck resisted democracy.

Looking now at the whole history of democratic progress, we see that the first setback occurred after the American Revolution when the supporters of democracy split into two camps, Jefferson's group advocating absolute democracy and Hamilton's group centralization of power in the government, and when the policy of centralization won out. The second setback occurred during the French Revolution when the people secured complete sovereignty but abused it and changed it into mob rule. The third setback occurred when Bismarck checked the people's power with his clever scheming. Democratic thought in the West has passed through these phases and has met these setbacks, yet, contrary to all expectation, it has of its own accord still moved forward and no human power has been able to thwart it or to hasten it. To-day democracy has become the great world problem, and the scholars of the world, whether conservative or progressive, all realize that the democratic idea cannot be suppressed. But as democracy develops, it will be inevitably abused in the same way as liberty and equality have been abused.

To sum up: the European and American

struggles for liberty and equality bore fruit in democracy: after democracy prevailed, it was much abused. Before the development of democracy, the Western nations tried to suppress it and to destroy it with autocratic power. When autocracy had been overthrown, the followers of democracy became the obstructionists of democracy. When democracy was realized, it produced many evils, and a greater obstacle thus resulted. Finally Bismarck saw that the people could not be downed in their desire for democracy, so he employed the power of the state as a substitute for the peoples' power and put into effect a state socialism; this policy also obstructed the march of democracy.

Tracing the beginnings of applied democracy, we see the American people after their revolution winning first the right to vote. At that time Westerners thought that democracy meant suffrage and that was all. If all the people without regard to social status, wealth, or intellectual capacity had the right to vote, democracy had reached its final goal. But what has been happening in the three or four years since the European War? In spite of many setbacks, democracy is still moving forward and cannot be checked. Recently the people of Switzerland have won, in addition to the right to vote, the right of initiative and referendum. If the people have the right to choose their officials, they should also have the right to initate and amend the laws. The rights of initiative and referendum are related to the enactment of laws. If a majority of the people think that a certain law will be beneficial, they can then propose it—this is the right of initiative; if they feel that a certain law is disadvantageous to them they can amend it—this is the right of referendum. The Swiss people have thus two more popular rights than other peoples, altogether three. Some of the newly developed states in the northwestern part of the United States have, in recent years, gained another right besides those of the Swiss people —the right of recall of officials. Although the enjoyment of this right is not universal throughout the United States, yet several states have practiced it, so many Americans enjoy the four popular rights—suffrage, recall, initiative and referendum. In some of the northwestern states they have been applied with great success, and some day they may be applied throughout the United States and perhaps throughout and world. In the future, any nation which wants complete democracy must certainly follow the example of these American states which have given four rights to the people. Do these four rights, when applied, fully solve the problems of democracy? World scholars, seeing that, although people have these four ideals of popular rights, yet the problem of democracy is not fully solved, say that it is only a matter of time. Ideas of direct popular rule, they consider, have developed but recently. The old theocracy lasted for tens of thousands of years; the old autocracy has lasted for thousands of years. This direct democracy is a very new thing; it has come only within the last few decades. No wonder it is still a great, unsettled issue!

What is the share of the people in the government in those nations which have the highest type of democracy? How much power do they possess? About the only achievement within the past century has been the right to elected and to be elected. After being elected as the representatives of the people, citizens can sit in Congress or Parliament to manage the affairs of state. All measures of national importance must be passed upon by Parliament before they can be put into effect; without Parliament's approval they cannot be carried out. This is called representative or parliamentary government. But does this form of government insure the perfect development of democracy? Before a representative system of government had been secured, the European and American peoples struggled for democracy, thinking that it would certainly be the highest type of popular sovereignty.

So the hope of foreigners that representative government will insure the stability and peace of the state is not to be trusted. Democracy as soon as it was born met with many difficulties; after it was applied it experienced many humiliations, but still it steadily grows. Yet the fruit of democracy has been only representative government; when this is achieved the nations think that the limit is reached.

But the democracy advocated in the Three Principles upon which the Kuomintang proposes to reconstruct China is different from Western democracy. When we use Western history as material for study, we are not copying the West entirely or following in its path. We will use our Principle of the People's Sovereignty and remake China into a nation under complete popular rule, ahead of Europe and America.

LECTURE FIVE

Delivered on March 16, 1924.

The Chinese people's ideas of political democracy have all come from the West, so in carrying forward our Revolution and in reforming our government we are imitating Western methods. Why? Because we see that Western civilization has been progressing by leaps and bounds, and that it is in every way more advanced than Chinese civiization.

Take other machinery which serves the needs of daily life and methods which are used in agriculture, industry, and business—the West has advanced far beyond China.

So, ever since the Boxer defeat,* Chinese thinkers have felt that, to make China strong and able to avenge the shame of the Peking Protocol, they must imitate foreign countries in

* 1900

everything. Not only must they learn material science from the West, but also political and social science. Thus, since the Boxer uprising the Chinese have lost all confidence in their own power, and a higher and higher respect has been paid to foreign countries. As a result of this imitation of and respect for foreign nations, China has taken in a lot or foreign ideas. Hence Chinese wanted nothing from old China; everything must be modeled after the West. If we heard of anything foreign, we ran to copy it and tried to use it in China. Democracy also met with this abuse. After the Revolution of 1911, the whole country went mad and insisted upon applying in China the political democracy which Westerners talked about, without any study of its real meaning. In the last few lectures I described in detail the history of the democratic struggle in the West and the results which followed the victory of democracy. From these studies we saw that democratic rule had not been fully carried out in the West and that democracy had met with many obstacles in its onward march. Now China is proposing to practice democracy. If we imitate the West, we will have to imitate Western methods. But there is no fundamental solution as yet in Western politics of the problem of democracy; it is still a serious issue. Westerners who are using the newest scholarship to aid them in finding a solution have not made any worth-while discoveries in democratic theory, nor have they found any satisfactory answer to the difficulties of democracy. So the methods of Western democracy cannot be our model or guide.

In the last two or three centuries, Europe and America have passed through many revolutions and their political progress has been much more rapid than China's, yet the Western political treatises do not show much advance upon the past. For instance, there lived in Greece two thousand years ago a great political philosopher named Plato; his *Republic* is still studied by scholars who say that it has much to contribute towards the political systems of to-day. It is not like battleships and drill manuals, which are discarded as worthless after ten years. From this we see that the physical sciences of the West undergo marked transformations from one decade to another; they are making rapid strides forward. But in the field of political theory, we find Plato's *Republic* written two millenniums ago still worthy of study and of great value in modern times. So the advance of Western political philosophy has not kept pace with the advance of Western material science. There has been no radical change in political thinking for two thousand years. If we copy Western government as we are copying Western material science, we shall be making a great mistake. The material civilization of the West is changing daily, and to keep up with it will be exceedingly difficult. But political thought in the West has advanced much more slowly than material civilization. The reason why Western democracy has not made more progress is that Western nations have not fundamentally solved the problem of administering democracy. We saw in the preceding lectures that the West has not yet found any proper method of carrying out democracy and that the truths of democracy have not yet been fully manifested. The democratic spirit has swollen like a noisy torrent within the last two or three centuries; in issues which men could not think through, the masses of the people have simply followed nature and have drifted with the tide. The recent growth of democracy is not an achievement of thoughtful scholarship but the result of a popular following of natural tendencies. For this reason, no fundamental method of directing democracy was worked out beforehand, the problem was not considered from beginning to end, and so the Western peoples have met innumerable disappointments and difficulties halfway on the road of democracy. Since the Revolution, China has wanted to follow the example of Europe and America and to apply political democracy. Since Western political democracy has developed to the point of representative government, China, too, must have a representative government! But the fine points of Western representative govermment China has not learned; the bad points she has copied tenfold, a hundredfold! China has not only failed to learn well from Western democratic government but has been corrupted by it.

From what I have already said, you must realize that Western democratic government does not have any fundamentally good method of application. So in our espousal of democracy, we should not entirely copy the West. Then what road shall we follow? For thousands of years Chinese social sentiments, customs, and habits have differed widely from those of Western society. Hence methods of social control in China are different from those used in the West, and we should not merely copy the West as we copy the use of their machinery. As soon as we learn Western machinery we can use it anytime, anywhere; electric lights, for example, can be installed and used in any kind of Chinese house. But Western social customs and sentiments are different from ours in innumerable points; if, without regard to customs and popular feelings in China, we try to apply Western methods of social control as we would Western machinery—in a hard and fast way—we shall be making a serious mistake. Hence this difference: in ways of controlling physical objects and forces we should learn from the West, but in ways of controlling men, we should not learn only from the West. The West long ago thought through the principles and worked out the methods of physical control, so we can wholly follow Western material civilization—we could even follow it blindly as we introduce it into China, and not go astray. But the West has not yet thought through its principles of government, and its methods of government have not been fundamentally worked out; so China to-day, when putting democracy into operation and reforming its government, cannot simply follow the West. We must think out a radically new method; if we only blindly follow others, we shall work serious injury to our national welfare and to the people's living. The West has its society; we have our society, and the sentiments and customs of the two are not the same. Only as we adapt ourselves, according to our own social conditions, to modern world tendencies, can we hope to reform our society and to advance our nation. If we pay no attention to our own social conditions and try simply to follow world tendencies, our nation will decline and our people will be in peril. If we want China to progress and our race to be safe, we must put democracy into effect ourselves and do some radical thinking upon the best way to realize its ideals.

Can we find a real way to carry out democratic government? Although we cannot wholly copy Europe and America, yet we can observe them and study their experience in democracy very carefully.

Foreign scholars, in studying the historical facts of democracy, have deduced many new theories. One of the newest has been proposed by an American scholar, who says that the greatest fear of modern democratic states is an all-powerful government which the people have no way of checking, but yet the finest thing would be an all-powerful government in the employ of all the people and working for the welfare of all the people. This is a very new theory: what is both feared and desired is an all-powerful government. First the theory declares that the people dread an all-powerful government which they cannot control, then it asks how an all-powerful government which will work for the welfare of the people can be secured, and how it can be made responsive to the will of the people. In many nations where democracy is developing, the governments are becoming powerless, while in the nations where democracy is weak, the governments are all strong. As I said before, the strongest government in Europe within the past few decades was Bismarck's government in Germany. That was certainly an all-powerful government; it did not advocate democracy, for at first it opposed democracy, but yet it became all-powerful. Of the governments which have supported democracy not one could be called all-powerful. A certain Swiss scholar has said that since various nations have put democracy into practice, the power of government has declined, and the reason has been the fear on the part of the people that the government might secure a power which they could not control. Hence the people have always guarded their governments and have not allowed them power, lest they become all-powerful. Therefore, democratic countries must find a solution for this difficulty, but the solution will not come until the people change their attitude towards government. The reason why the people have always been opposing government is because, after the revolutions, the liberty and equality thus obtained were overdeveloped, and certain groups abused them, setting no limits upon them and going into all sorts of excess, with the result that the government became impotent, and the state, although it had a government, became no different from a state without a government. The Swiss scholar whom I mentioned saw this evil train of events, and as a remedy proposed that the people should change their attitude towards government. What did he mean? What has the attitude of the people to do with government?

In China's long history, what has been the attitude of the people towards the government? As we study Chinese history, we find that the governments of Yao, Shun, Yu, T'ang, Wen Wang, and Wu Wang* are always lauded and held in admiration by the Chinese people; Chinese of every period hoped that they might have a government like those, which would seek the welfare of the people. Before Western democratic ideas penetrated China, the deepest desire of the Chinese people was for emperors like Yao, Shun, Yu, T'ang, Wen Wang, and Wu Wang, that the people might

* Emperors of ancient China.

enjoy peace and happiness. this was the old Chinese attitude towards government. But since our recent revolution, the people have absorbed democratic ideas and are no longer satisfied with those ancient emperors. They were all autocratic rulers, the people say, and do not deserve to be extolled even though they were splendid. This shows that the rise of democracy has developed an attitude of opposition to government among the people; no matter how good the government is, they are not content with it. If we let this attitude of mind continue without any attempt to change it, it will be exceedingly difficult for government to make any progress.

When we launched our revolution, we advocated the practice of democracy; and I have thought of a method to solve the problem. The method which I have thought of is a new discovery in political theory and is a fundamental solution of the whole problem. My proposition is similar to the thesis of the Swiss scholar that the attitude of people to government must be changed, and the recent appearance of such theories in the West proves that the principle which I have advocated is right; namely, that a distinction should be made between sovereignty and ability*. Western scholars have not yet discovered this principle. To make clear what I mean, I must first review my theory as to the classes of human society.

Upon what did I base my division of human society?—Upon the individual's natural intelligence and ability. I classified mankind into three groups. The first group are those who see and perceive first: they are the people of superior wisdom who take one look at a thing and see numerous principles involved, who hear one word and immediately perform great deeds, whose insight into the future and

* *Ch'uan and Nen* are difficult to translate by one phrase because of the various shades of meaning in different contexts. They convey the idea of "right" and "power" as well as "sovereignty" and "ability" and might be so rendered.

whose many achievements make the world advance and give mankind its civilization. These men of vision and foresight are the creators, the discoverers of mankind. The second group includes those who see and perceive later: their intelligence and ability are below the standard of the first group; they cannot create or discover but can only follow and imitate, learning from what the first group have already done. The third group are those who do not see or perceive: they have a still lower grade of inelligence and ability and do not understand even though one tries to teach them; they simply act. In the language of political movements, the first group are the discoverers; the second group, the promoters; the third group, the operators. Progress in everything depends upon action, so the responsibility for the world's progress rests upon the third group.

For example, the construction of a large foreign-style building is not something which can be undertaken by the ordinary person. First there must be a construction engineer, who makes a complete estimate of the work and materials necessary for the desired building, and then draws a detailed plan for the contractor or foreman. The foreman first studies the plan carefully, then hires workmen to move materials and to work according to the plan. The workmen cannot read the plan; they merely work according to the foreman's directions and take his orders to put a brick here or to lay a tile there—simple tasks. The foreman, in turn, is unable to make complete estimates on the building or to draw a plan; he can only follow the plan made by the construction engineer and give orders to the workmen as to the laying of the brick and covering with tile. The construction engineer who designs the plan is the one who sees and perceives first; the foreman who reads the plan is the one who sees and perceives afterward, the workman who lays brick and tile is the one who does not see or perceive. The foreign buildings in every city depend upon these groups—engineers, foremen, and workmen—and upon their cooperative effort. All the great achievements of the world also depend upon these three groups, but the largest group is the one of practical operators who do not know or perceive. A smaller group are those who know and perceive afterward; the smallest group are those who know and perceive first. Without men who see and perceive ahead, the world would have no originators: without men who see and perceive later, the world would have no supporters; without men who do not see or perceive, the world would have no practical workers. The business of the world certainly requires first, initiators; next, many promoters; and lastly, a large number of operators, in order to be successfully accomplished. the process of the world depends on these three types, and not one type must be lacking. The nations of the world, as they begin to apply democracy and to reform the government, should give a part to every man—to the man who sees first, to the man who sees later, to the man who does not see. We must realize that political democracy is not given to us by nature; it is created by human effort. We must create democracy and then give it to the people, not wait to give it until the people fight for it.

Since the West has not solved the difficulties of democracy, we cannot find a solution to-day by merely copying the West. We must look for a new way, and that new way depends, as the Swiss scholar said, upon a change of attitude towards government. But to secure this change of attitude we must distinguish clearly between sovereignty and ability. To help us in studying this distinction, let us review a few of the points mentioned in a former lecture. The first point is our definition of the people's sovereignty; briefly, it means the control of the government by the people. To explain this further: who controlled the government in former times? Two ancient Chinese sayings, "One who does not hold a position under the government does not concern himself with the government" and "The common people are not in the councils," show that political sovereignty used to be entirely in the hands of the emperor and had nothing to do with the people. To-day we who advocate democracy want to put the political sovereignty into the hands of the people. What, then, will the people become? Since China has had a revolution and has adopted a democratic form of government, the people should rule in all matters. The government now may be called popular government; in other words, under a republic we make the people king.

Looking back through the millenniums of Chinese history, the only emperors who shouldered the responsibility of government for the welfare and happiness of the people were Yao, Shun, Yu, T'ang, Wen Wang, and Wu Wang; no others were able to use their office for the blessing of the people. Of all China's emperors, only Yao, Shun, Yu, T'ang, Wen Wang, and Wu Wang so fulfilled their duties of government that they could stand "unabashed before

Heaven above and unashamed before men below." They were able to reach this high ideal and to elicit pæans of praise from succeeding generations because of two special qualities which they possessed—fine native ability, which enabled them to establish good government and to seek the welfare of the people; and noble character, "mercy to the people and kindness to all creatures, regard for the people as for the wounded and suffering, love for the people as for their own children." Because they possessed these two fine qualities, they were able to shoulder the full responsibility of the government and to reach their goal. These are the only emperors who have called forth reverence from posterity. Other emperors there have been—we do not know how many—and most of them, with their names, have been forgotten by posterity. Only Yao, Shun, Yu, T'ang, Wen Wang, and Wu Wang possessed great natural ability and noble character. Most of the others lacked ability and character, yet they wielded sovereign power.

You have all read a good deal of Chinese history; I am sure almost everyone here has read particularly *The Story of the Three Kingdoms.** We can find an illustration of our point in this book. Chukuh Liang, You remember, was a very scholarly and able statesman. The first chief that he served was Liu Pei; later he supported Ah Tou. Ah Tou was exceedingly stupid and did not have a bit of ability, which was the reason why Liu Pei just before his death said to Chukuh Liang, "If he is deserving of your support, support him; otherwise you may displace him." After Liu Pei's death, Chukuh Liang still showed his splended character; although Ah Tou was worthless, Chukuh Liang aided him as loyally as ever, "wearing himself out with the duties of his office until he died." Thus, in the age of autocracy the ruler might have no ability but great power. Ah Tou and Chukuh Liang, in the period of the Three King-

* The period of three Kingdoms, A. D. 122-265 was rich in military heroes and deeds of valor and has been immortalized by this well-known voluminous novel.

doms, make this very clear to us: Chukuh Liang had ability but not power; Ah Tou had power but not ability. Ah Tou was incompetent, but he turned the affairs of state over to Chukuh Liang to administer. Chukuh Liang was exceedingly capable and so was able to build up a fine government in Western Shu (modern Szechwan); moreover, he was able to lead his troops six times across the Ch'i Mountains in a punitive expedition against the North and to establish a tripod of power along with the Wei and Wu kingdoms. The comparison between Chukuh Liang and Ah Tou helps us to understand the distinction between sovereignty and ability.

In the age of autocracy fathers and elder brothers were kings, sons and younger brothers were heirs. A1though they might have no ability at all, yet they could become kings some day. So incompetent men still had great sovereign power. Now that we have established a republic and acknowledge the people as ruler, will you look about to see to what groups our four hunderd millions belong? Of course they cannot all be seers; most of them are not even follows of seers; the great majority are those who have no vision or foresight. Now democratic government depends upon the rulership of the people, hence our four hundred millions are very powerful. The people of the nation with sovereign power to control the government are these very four hundred millions. To whom can you compare all these political sovereigns? I think that they are very much like Ah Tou. In fact, each one of them is an Ah Tou with great sovereign power. Ah Tou had no ability, but Chukuh Liang did; so after Liu Pei's death, Western Shu was still well governed. Westerners now are opposing a powerful government; the Swiss scholar, to remedy this defect, proposes that the people's attitude towards government should be changed—they should no longer be hostile to strong government. But what the next step is, after the popular attitude towards government is changed, they have not made clear. The principle which I am bringing out is that sovereignty must be distinguished from ability; without this clear distinction we cannot hope to change the people's attitude towards government. Ah Tou knew that he was incompetent, so he turned over all the political authority of the kingdom to Chukuh Liang and ask Chukuh Liang to govern for him. So when Chukuh Liang handed in his memorandum upon the expedition to Ah Tou, he advised him to separate clearly the affairs of the palace and the affairs of the court. Ah Tou could execute the duties of the palace, but the duties of the court he could not perform alone, for they were duties of government. chukuh Liang's distinction between palace and court was a distinction between sovereignty and ability. In governing the state, we must make the same distinction. How shall we do it? We shall succeed only as we take a long and dispassionate view of world affairs. Everybody now has a peculiar idea of government which has grown up out of millenniums of autocracy. In this long period of autocratic government, incompetent men have sat upon the throne while the four hunderd millions have been their slaves; now, although autocracy is overthrown, a republic is established, and we are apparently free, yet the people have not gotten rid of their idea of autocracy and are still afraid that the government will oppress them as the emperors did. The fear of an imperial, despotic government makes them want to destroy the government and the attitude of hostility towards government develops. This present hostility is still the reaction from the old reverence for the emperor. In other words, from an attitude of extreme veneration for the emperor the people have swung to an attitude of opposition towards all government. The old worship of the emperor was wrong, of course, but the present hostility to all government is also wrong.

We must go back thousands of years in political history in order to understand how this wrong conception to-day can be broken down. Before the day of despotic emperors, China had the splendid rulers Yao and Shun; they both opened the throne to the people and did not attempt to keep it in their own family. Autocracy did not flower until after Yao and Shun; before their time there was no autocracy to speak of, and men of ability who could work for the welfare of all and organize good government were appointed emperors. In the wild age of conflict between men and beasts, which we formerly described, there was no complete state organization; the people lived by clans and depended upon some skillful and strong man to provide for their protection. At that time people were afraid of the attack of venomous serpents and wild beasts, so they had to get an able man to assume the responsibility for protection. Responsibility for protection required ability to fight; the man who could overcome venomous serpents and savage beasts was considered the ablest, and, as men of that day had no weapons but bare hands and empty fists with which to fight, the one with the strongest body was raised by the people to the position of chief. China, however, had examples of others besides fighters who were made kings. Sui Jen Shih* bored wood for fire and taught the people to cook with fire; thus the dangers of eating raw vegetables and meat were avoided and many fine flavors to satisfy the palate were discovered. So the people made Sui Jen Shih king. Boring wood for fire and teaching people to cook with fire were the work of a cook, so we may say that a cook became king. Shen Nung* tasted a hundred herbs and discovered many medicinal properties to heal diseases and to raise the dead to life—a wonderful and meritorious work—so they made him king. Tasting herbs is the work of a physician, and thus we may say that a physician became king. Hsien Yuan* taught the people to make clothes, so it was the tailor who became king; Yu Ch'ao Shih* taught the people how to build houses, and so the carpen-

* Lcgcndary figures in ancient Chinese history.

ter became king. So in Chinese history we find not only those who could fight becoming king; anyone with marked ability, who had made new discoveries or who had achieved great things for mankind, could become king and organize the government. Cooks, physicians, tailors, carpenters, and all others who had special ability had become king. The general psychology of the Chinese is that a man possessing marked ability should become king.

Since the time of Yao and Sun China's emperors have gradually become despots, wanting to monopolize the empire and refusing to let the people freely choose able men for the throne. If now our four hundred million people should be asked to elect an emperor by ballot, if they had complete power and freedom of choice without any outside interference, and if, at the same time, Yao and Shun should come to life again, whom do you think they would elect? I think they would undoubtedly elect Yao or Shun. Chinese have not the painful and bitter feelings towards their emperors which Westerners have had, because despotism in China was never as severe as despotism in the West. In Europe two or three centuries ago the tyranny of kings had reached its limits: the people looked upon thier rulers as they would upon an overwhelming deluge or a savage beast—with mortal terror. So the people wanted to reject not only thier kings but everything closely connected with kings, such as government. Now that democracy prevails in the West and the people are in power, the rejection of government is truly easy. Would it not have been easy for Ah Tou of Western Shu to throw Chukuh Liang overboard? But if he had dismissed Chukuh Liang, could the government of Western Shu have lasted very long, could the troops have been dispatched six times across the Ch'i Mountains to punish the North? Ah Tou realized all this, so he gave complete authority to Chukuh Liang; the setting in order of the government, the suppression of the South, the punitive expedition gainst the

North, were all carried out by Chukuh Liang. We are now putting democracy into practice: the four hundred millions of China are the kings; they are the Ah Tous, and as Ah Tous they should naturally welcome Chukuh Liang to administer the government for them and to perform the great tasks of state. As Western nations have applied democracy, the people have developed an attitude of hostility towards government, and the fundamental reason is their failure to distinguish between sovereignty and ability. Unless we act upon this principle which I have set forth, we will simply follow in the ruts of the West. Only as the people, in accordance with the theory that I have set forth, see the clear difference between sovereignty and ability will hostility towards government cease and will government have a chance to develop. It should be very easy for China to make the distinction, for we can cite the precedent of Ah Tou and Chukuh Liang. If the government is a good one, we four hundred millions will let it be our Chukuh Liang and give all the authority of the state to it; if the government is bad, we four hundred millions can exercise the privileges of kingship, dismiss it and take back the authority into our own hands. Westerners have not drawn a clear line between sovereignty and ability, so they have not yet solved the problems which have arisen out of democracy these two or three hundred years.

Let us make another comparison between the past and the present. In olden times those who could fight well were crowned king by all. To-day, when wealthy men organize a company or open a factory, they have to engage a man with natural capability to be general manager and to control the concern. This general manager is an expert who has the ability; the shareholders hold the authority or sovereignty. within the factory, only the general manager gives orders; the shareholders simply keep a supervision over him. The people of a republic are shareholders, the president is general manager, and the people should look upon the government as an expert. With such an attitude, the shareholders can make use of the manager to improve the factory, turn out a large quantity of goods with a small capital, and make large profits for the company. But in none of the democratic states of the West do the people have such an attitude towards government, hence they cannot make use of gifted men to direct the government. As a result, the men in political life are generally incompetent, and democratic government is developing very haltingly. The reason lies in their failure to solve some of the basic problems of democracy. To solve them they must put the important affairs of the nation in the hands of capable men.

Westerners to-day are constantly making use of experts: in training soldiers they use experienced military men, in running their factories they use engineers, and in the administration of government they know that they ought to use specialists. They have not succeeded in doing so because they are not able to change the old, deep-rooted habits of the people. But in this new age a distinction must surely be made between sovereignty and ability. In many things we have to trust experts and we should not set limitations upon them. Take that very recent invention, now in such common use and so convenient—the automobile. When automobiles were first introduced twenty or thirty years ago, there were no expert chauffeurs to drive them or expert mechanics to repair them. I had a friend who bought an automobile and had to be both chauffeur and mechanic himself, which was a lot of trouble, as one could not be expected to do all these things well. But now there are many chauffeurs and mechanics, and the owner of an automobile has only to pay out money and engage someone to drive or to repair his car for him. The chauffeurs and the mechanics are specialists in driving and in repair work, and they are essential if we use automobiles. The nation is a great automobile and the government officers are the great chauffeurs. When Westerners first won political sovereignty, they wre like the wealthy owners of automobiles twenty years age, who did not have suitable experts to help them and so had to do all the repairing and driving themselves. But now that there are so many gifted specialists, the sovereign people should engage their services; to drive and repair by themselves is only "seeking worry and trouble." In this illustration we can make a distinction, also, between the chauffeur who has skill but not sovereignty over the car, and the owner of the car who has sovereignty but not skill. The sovereign owner should depend upon the skillful expert to drive his car, and the same principle should apply in the vital affairs of the nation. The people are the owners; they must be sovereign. The government are specialists; they must be men of ability and skill. We are therefore to look upon all the officers of the government, from president and premier down to heads of departments, as specially trained chauffeurs; if they are able men and loyal to the nation, we should be willing to give the sovereignty of the state into their hands. We must not limit their movements but give them freedom of action; then the state can progress and progress with rapid strides. If, on the contrary, we attempt to take everything into our own hands, or to hamper our experts at every turn and not allow them freedom of action, the state can hardly hope to progress much and will move forward very slowly.

I can give you a very good illustration of this principle out of my own experience. Once, when I was living in Shanghai, I made an appointment for a conference with a friend in Hongkow. But when the day came, I forgot the appointment until just fifteen minutes before that set time. I was then living in the French concession, which is a long distance from Hongkow. It would be almost impossible to get there in fifteen minutes. In hot haste I called a chauffeur and asked him excitedly whether he could drive to Hongkow in fifteen minutes. He replied that he certainly could. so I took my seat in the automobile and we started for the appointed place. I was very familiar with the streets of Shanghai; the trip from the French concession to Hongkow is somewhat like that from Shakee to Tungshan (in Canton) which you can cut short by going through the Bund and Ch'uan Lung K'ou. But my chauffeur did not go, let us say, by the Bund and Ch'uan Lung K'on; he first went down Fungning Road, turned through Taoteksun Road, and drove through the small North Gate before he reached the Great East Gate and then Tungshan. The automobile was flying along and making such a noise that I could not speak to the chauffeur; I was much puzzled, however, and angry at the chauffeur, because I thought he was playing a trick on me and deliberately going out of the way to extend the time. The situation was similar to that in a nation when the government, for a special reason, does something extraordinary which the people do not understand, and the people misinterpret it and find fault. But that chauffeur, going by the route he had chosen, reached Hongkow in not over fifteen minutes. My indignation cooled and I asked the chauffeur why he had come by such a circuitous route. He replied, "If we had taken the direct route, we would have driven along the Nanking Road where traffic is heavy with street cars, automobiles, jinrickshas, pedestrians, and moving vans, and where it is difficult to get through." This cleared up my misunderstanding; I realized that the way I had planned through Nanking Road and over the Garden Bridge at the Bund was conceived only in terms of distance, but the chauffeur had experience. He knew that an automobile could travel very fast, thirty or forty miles an hour, and that a few more turns and a few more miles with the chance, however, of increasing the speed, would still put us at our destination within the appointed time. He calculated directly from the time; he was not a philosopher and did not understand the formal relations of time and space, but he was a specialist in his line. He knew that an automobile has the power of shortening distance, and that if he could increase the speed of the car a few more turns would nor prevent him from reaching Hongkow within fifteen minutes. If I had not given the chauffeur complete authority and allowed him freedom of movement, but had insisted that he take my route, I certainly could not have kept my engagement. Because I trusted him as an expert and did not bind his arm, he was able to take that route which he thought was best, and arrived at the appointed time. But since I was not an expert, I misunderstood why he should go out of the direct way. The people are masters of the nation and should act towards the government as I did towards the chauffeur on that ride to Hongkow, that is, let it drive and choose the way. Only such a conception of government will change the attitude of people towards government.

The hostility of Western peoples towards their governments is due to their failure to separate sovereignty from ability, and consequently they have not yet cleared up the difficulties of democracy. Let us not, as we pursue democracy, copy the West; let us make a clear distinction between sovereignty and ability. Although the democratic ideas came to us from Europe and America, yet the administration of democracy has not been successfully worked out there. We know a way now to make use of democracy and we know how to change the attitude of people towards government, but yet the majority of the people are without vision. We who have prevision must lead them and guide them into the right way if we want to escape the confusions of Western democracy and not follow in the tracks of the West. Western scholars to-day have only gotten to the point of realizing that the attitude of the people towards government is wrong and ought to be changed, but they do not yet see how to change it. I have now discovered the way we must distinguish between sovereignty and ability. The foundation of the government of a nation must be built upon the rights of the people, but the administration of government mnst be intrusted to experts. We must not look upon these experts as stately and grand presidents and ministers, but simply as our chauffeurs, as guards at the gate, as cooks, physicians, carpenters, or tailors. It does not matter what sort of workmen the people consider them. As long as they have this general attitude towards them, the state can be governed and the nation can go forward.

LECTURE SIX

Delivered on April 26, 1924.

Western statesmen and students of jurisprudence now speak of government as machinery and of law as an instrument. A great many Chinese books on government and law are translations from the Japanese; the Japanese have given government organization the designation of *chi-kuan* (organ, or bureau). *Chi-kuan* means the same thing as the common word "machinery" in China; when we say *chi-kuan* we mean the same thing as machinery, an adminstrative organ may, therefore, be called administrative machinery. But what is the difference between political machinery and manufacturing machinery? Manufacturing machinery is made entirely of material things wood, steel, leather belts, and such-fitted together; politcal machinery is constucted of human beings and depends upon human beings, not material things, for its action. So there are great differences between political and manufacturing machinery, but the one that stands out is the fact that political machinery is moved by human forces, while manufacturing machinery is moved by material forces.

Western civilization and culture have been developing and progressing with great rapidity. But when we analyze this progress we find that material civilization, as represented by manufacturing machinery, has been advancing very rapidly, while human machinery, as seen in political organization, has made very slow advance. What is the reason for this? When material machinery is constructed, it can be easily tried out, the bad features can be discarded, and the imperfect parts can be improved. But after human machinery has been set up, it is not easily experimented with and improvements are not at all easily made, except through revolution. The only other way would be to treat it as scrap iron, as we do old material machinery, but this is manifestly impossible. Hence manufacturing machinery in the West has progressed by leaps and bounds, while political machinery has just stumbled along. There is nothing over ten years old among the machines used in modern agriculture, industry, and business; for every decade brings numerous inventions and improvements and every year marks some advance. Yet the political machinery of a hundred years ago is still in use to-day. The individual human beings in this machinery of human forces can change at will, but the whole organization is not easily reconstructed from the bottom up because of deep-seated habits and the close sequence of life activities. Without some sort of revolution, it is impossible in ordinary times to discard entirely the old organization. This explains the rapid advance of material machinery in the West, while political machinery advanced so slowly and with such difficulty.

In two former lectures, I said that Westerners had not yet found a fundamental method of procedure in carrying out democratic government. This is because they have not experimented carefully and skillfully with their political machinery. Between the first inventions of material machinery and the machinery we see to-day there have been we know not how many thousands of experiments and improvements. This led to our modern automatic machines. The machinery of democratic government, after more than a hundred years, is limited to the power of voting; there has been no advance beyond this stage for a long time. There is no other way of controlling the men who are elected to office, whether they turn out to be worthy or incompetent. Such a condition is due to imperfections in the machinery of democracy, and consequently democratic government has not yet found a good mode of procedure and has made but little progress. If we want to improve the machinery, what shall we do? As I said in my previous lecture, we must make a clear distinction between sovereignty and ability.

Statesmen and students of jurisprudence are now speaking of government as a machine and of law as an instrument, and our modern democratic age looks opon the people as the motive power in government. In the old autocratic age the king was the motive power and all the activities of the state were initiated by him. The greater the power of the government, the greater the majesty of the throne. A strong government was essential for the effective carrying out of the imperial edicts. Since the king was the power behind the machinery, a strong government organization made it possible for the king, in his exalted position, to do whatever he pleased—initiate political reforms, carry on "long-range aggressions," prepare for war, or anything else. So in the age of autocracy, increased power in the government brought advantage but no injury to the king. But in the age of democracy, people are the motive power in government. Then why are they loath to have too strong a government? Because if the government is too powerful they cannot control it and will be oppressed by it. Because they were once excessively oppressed by their government and suffered so much from it, they are trying to prevent oppression in the future by limiting the power of government. These are the early days of democracy and our methods of controlling government are also defective. The people are naturally the motive power in a democracy, but the people must also be able at any time to recall the power they set loose. Therefore the people will use only a low-powered government, for they cannot control a government of several hundred thousand horse power and will not dare to use it. The fear of powerful government among Western peoples to-day is just like the fear of powerful machinery in the old factories. As for their political machinery, however, the people are not thinking of ways to improve it and are fearful of giving it too much power lest they be unable to call the power back. Instead, they are constantly thinking of ways to limit the government until it has no chance to develop and democracy has no chance to advance. Looking at present tendencies in the world, we may say that there is steady progress in democratic ideas but no progress at all in the control of democratic government. This is the reason why Western democratic nations have not found as yet a fundamental method of procedure.

As I have said in my preceding lecture, we must make a distinction between sovereignty and ability. When we apply this distinction to the illustration of the machine, where do we place the ability or power? The machine itself is what possesses the ability or power. A 100,000 horse power machine, fed with the proper amount of coal and water, will generate the proper ability and power. Where is the sovereignty? The engineer in control of the machine possesses the sovereignty. No matter what the horse power of the machine, the engineer has only to move his hand and machine will start and start immediately or stop and stop immediately. The engineer can control the machine, and make it do as he wishes; as soon as the machine starts, he can make the steamship or the train go very fast, and by stopping the machine he can make the steamer or the train cease moving. The machine, then, is an able and powerful thing, while the engineer is a man with a large degree of sovereignty. If the people in their control of government will make a distinction between sovereignty and ability or power, they will be like the engineer who controls the great machinery. When democracy is highly developed and methods of controlling government are perfected, the government will have great power, but the people will only have to make their opinions known in their national congress; if they attack the government, they may overthrow it, or if they laud the government they may strenghten it. But as it is, if the government carries on with a high hand, the people have no way to control it, no matter how much the people may criticize or praise the government, their words are ineffective and the government pays no attention to them. To-day government is making no progress, while the democratic spirit flourishes. The people of all countries are finding that the present political machinery does not suit their ideas or needs.

China now is in a period of revolution. We are advocating a democratic form of government. Our ideas of democracy have come from the West. We have recently been thinking how we might copy these ideas and build up a nation under popular government. When we were first considering this kind of state, one group of revolutionary enthusiasts believed that if we would imitate the West exactly, follow right in the tracks of the West, and copy everything from the West, then Chinese democracy would develop to the limit of perfection. At first such ideas were not entirely wrong, for China's old autocratic government was so corrupt that if we could, after effecting a revolution and overthrowing the autocracy, begin our constructive effort by learning from the West, we should certainly be better off than under the old regime. But are the peoples of the West thoroughly satisfied with the present situation in their national and social life? If we will make a careful study of Western government and society, we shall find that in the so-called pioneer revolutionary states, like the United States and France, people are still proposing improvements in government and are still thinking of revolution. Why, when they had revolutions a century ago, are they thinking of other revolutions? This proves that we were wrong when we thought that following the West would lead us to the heights of perfection; and if we should fully copy the United States and France, which are still contemplating revolution, we could not escape another revolution a hundred years hence. For the governmental machinery of the United States and France still has many defects, and does not satisfy the desires of the people nor give them a complete measure of happiness. So we in our proposed reconstruction must not think that if we imitate the West of to-day we shall reach the last stage of progress and be perfectly contented. If we follow the dust of the West, will not each generation be more dissatisfied than the one previous, and will we not finally have to stage another revolution? If another revolution is going to be necessary, then is not this one a vain effort? What shall we do to keep this revolution from being a futile waste of energy? What plans shall we lay in order to secure a permanent government and a lasting peace—"enduring repose after one supreme effort"—and prevent calamities in the future ?

Can we bring over the methods of the West and apply them wholesale in China?

As I said in a former lecture, Europe and America have not gone to the bottom in their study of the problems of democracy, and consequently the people are in daily conflict with their governments. The force of democracy is new, but the machinery of democracy is old. If we want to solve the difficulties of democracy we must build another machinery, a new machinery, upon the principle that sovereignty and ability are different things. The people must have sovereignty, the machinery must have ability and power. Modern efficient and powerful machinery is operated by men who can start and stop it at will. The West has made the most complete inventions in the field of machinery but very imperfect discoveries in the field of government. If we want to make a complete change in government, we have no model to follow but must discover a new way for ourselves. Are we able to do such a thing? Since the Boxer year, Chinese have completely lost their self-confidence. The attitude of the people is one of absolute faith in foreign countries and distrust of themselves. That they should accomplish anything of themselves or make any original discovery seems to them impossible. No, they must run after the West and copy Western ways. We do not see that Western civilization is strong only in its material aspects and not in its various political aspects. From the standpoint of scientific theories of a material Civilization, Europe and America have developed remarkably in recent years. But because a man is outstanding in one field of knowledge does not necessarily signify that he is equally proficient in all fields of knowledge; in many of them he may even be blind. Their physical sciences have developed to the highest point in the past century and their many new inventions have "usurped the powers of Nature" beyond our wildest dreams. But to say that what they have not thought of in political science we cannot think of or discover is unreasonable. Western machinery has indeed made much progress in recent times, but this does not prove that Western political systems have progressed also. For two or more centuries the specialty of the West has been only science. The great scientists are naturally well advanced in their own branches of knowledge, but this does not necessarily make them equally advanced in all branches of knowledge.

Western science has progressed to the point of making material machinery automatically double-acting, but the people's sovereignty over the government is still single-acting; it can only be advanced and not taken back. While we are advocating democracy for the reconstruction of our republic, let us have a thoroughgoing new democracy and a thoroughgoing new republic. If we should not wholly follow the advanced states of the West, we should think out a new and better procedure ourselves. Are we capable of doing this? For thousands of years China has been an independent country. In our former political development, we never borrowed materials from other countries. China had one of the earliest civilizations in the world and never needed to copy wholly from others. Only in recent times has Western culture advanced beyond ours, and the passion for this new civilization has stimulated our revolution. Now that the revolution is a reality, we naturally desire to see China excel the West and build up the newest and most progressive state in the world. We certainly possess the qualifications necessary to reach this ideal, but we must not merely imitate the democratic systems of the West. These systems have become old-style machinery.

To reach our ideal we must construct a new machinery. Is there any material in the world for such a new machinery? Yes, there is much material scattered in various countries, but we must first decide upon a fundamental line of procedure. And this line of procedure is the separation of sovereignty and ability which I have already discussed. Then, as we put democracy into operation, we must separate the organization of the state and the administration of democracy. Western nations have not thought through these basic principles and have not distinguished between sovereignty and power or ability, consequently their government's power does not expand. Now that we have thought through our basic principle, we must go a step further and divide the machinery of government. In order to do this, we must understand well the idea of government. In Lecture One, I gave a definition for government—a thing of and by all the people and control of the affairs of all the people. The government machinery which is constructed according to the principle of sovereignty being distinct from ability and power is just like material machinery which has power in itself and is controlled by a power outside. In building the new state according to the newest discoveries, we should separate clearly these two kinds of power. But how? We must start from the meaning of government. Government or politics is a concern of all the people, and its centralizing force is political sovereignty. Political sovereignty, then means popular sovereignty, and government which centralizes the forces controlling the life of the people is called government power or government authourity.

There are, then, two forces in politics, the political power of the people and the administrative power of the government. One is the power of control, the other is the power of the government itself. What does this mean? A steamship has a 100,000 horse power engine: the generation of 100,000 horse power and the moving of the vessel are in the power of the machinery itself, and this power may be compared to the power of the government. But the movement of the great steam vessel forward and backward, to the right or left, its stopping, and its rate of speed, all depend upon the control of a good engineer. He is essential to the direction and control of a perfect machine; by perfect control the powerful vessel can be made to start and to stop at will. This power of control may be compared to the control over government, which is political sovereignty. Building a new state is like building a new steamship. If we put in low-powered machinery, the speed of the vessel will naturally be low, its freight capacity will be small, and profits from its running meager. But if we install high-powered machinery, the vessel will have a high rate of speed, will be able to carry heavy freight, and will bring in large profits. If we could build a steamship with a speed of 50 knots, then no other steamship could compete with it, and we would have the fastest and largest new steamship in the world. The same principle applies in the building of a state. If we construct a low-powered, weak government, its activities will be limited and its accomplishments will be meager. But if we put in a high-powered, strong government, its activities will be broad in scope and it will accomplish great things. If a powerful government should be installed in the largest state in the world, would not that state outstrip all others? Would not that government be unequaled under heaven?

Why have the nations of the West

steamships with high-powered machinery but not states with high-powered strong governments? Because they can only control high-powered machinery, but have not found a way to control high-powered government. To discard a low-powered old vessel and build a high-powered new one is an easy task; but the state has very deep roots and the construction of a new powerful government in place of an old weak government is a very difficult thing. China with her four hundred million people is the most populous state in the world; her territory is broad and her products are rich and abundant, exceeding those of the United States. The United States has now become the wealthiest and most powerful nation in the world, and no other nation can compare with her. When we compare our natural resources, it seems that China should outstrip the United States, but as a matter of fact, not only is this impossible now but the two countries cannot even be mentioned in the same breath. The reason is that the Chinese have the necessary qualifications but want human effort. We have never had a real good government. But if we add human effort to our natural qualifications, build up a complete, strong government which will display great power and move the whole nation, then China can immediately begin to advance in line with the United States.

After China secures a powerful government, we must not be afraid, as Western peoples are, that the government will become too strong and out of control. Because our plan for the reconstructed state includes the division of the political power of the whole state into two parts. The political power will be given into the hands of the people, who will have a full degree of sovereignty and will be able to control directly the affairs of state; this political power is popular sovereignty. The other power is government, and we will put that entirely in the government organs, which will be powerful and will manage all the nation's business; this political power is the power of government. If the people have a full measure of political sovereignty and the methods for exercising popular control over the government are well worked out, we need not fear that the government will become too powerful and uncontrollable. Westerners formerly did not dare to build machines with over 100,000 horse power; because machines were not perfectly constructed and the means of control were not compact, they were afraid of their power and would not risk the control of them. But now such wonderful improvements have been made in machinery, the machines themselves are so well constructed and the control mechanism is so compact, that Westerners are building machines with tremendous horse power. If we want to build a much-improved political machinery, we must follow the same line: we must have a complete and powerful government organ, and at the same time have a compact method of popular sovereignty to exercise control over the government organ. Western governments lack this compact and effective control, so they are not yet making much progress. Let us not follow in their tracks. Let the people in thinking about government distinguish between sovereignty and power. Let the great political force of the state be divided; first let there be the power of the government and then the power of the peoople. Such a division will make the government the machinery and the people the engineer. The attitude of the people towards their government will then be like the attitude of the engineer towards his machinery.

Such advances have been made in the construction of machinery that not only men with mechanical knowledge, but even children without any knowledge of machinery can control it.

China has now the idea of democracy, but no perfect machinery has yet been invented in the world to express this idea. The people do not know how to to use it. We who have vision and foresight must first build the machine. We must construct a very serviceable kind of faucet, a very safe kind of electric button which ordinary people can learn how to use by a single turn of the hand; then the idea of democracy will become a reality. What methods shall we use in applying the democracy which we have adopted from the West? Only after we have thought through these methods will democracy be adapted to our use. If we insist on using democracy without careful preparation beforehand, we will find it extremely dangerous and liable to kill us. Have such methods of applying democracy yet been found? Switzerland in Europe has some partial methods which she has already tried out; they are radical and give the people direct sovereignty, but are not very complete. The larger nations of Europe have not even experimented with these incomplete methods. The fact that only the small state of Switzerland has tried a partial form of direct sovereignty makes many people question whether it is applicable in large states also. Why are not the large states using Switzerland's methods? Because they "fear difficulties and seek ease," these advanced people, though familiar with the newly invented models, do not make use of them. But we in China never had any old machinery of democracy, so we ought to be able to choose and use the newest and best discoveries.

What are the newest discoveries in the way of applying democracy? First, there is the suffrage, and it is the only method in operation throughout the so-called modern democracies. Is this one form of popular sovereignty enough in government? This one power by itself may be compared to the early machines which could move forward only but not back. The second of the newly discovered methods is the power of recall. With this power, the people can pull the machine back. These two rights, the right to elect and the right to recall give the people control over their officials and enable them to put all government officials in their positions or to move them out of their positions. The coming and going of officials follows the free will of the people just as modern machines move to and fro by the free action of the engine. Another important thing in a state, in addition to officials, is law; "with men to govern there must also be ways of governing." What power must the people possess in order to control the laws? If all the people think that a certain law would be of great advantage to them, they should have the power to decide upon this law and turn it over to the government for execution. This third kind of popular power is called the initiative. If everybody thinks that an old law is not beneficial to the people, they should have the power to amend it and to ask the government to administer the revised law and do away with the old law. This is called the referendum and is a fourth form of popular sovereignty. Only when the people have these four powers can we say that there is a full measure of democracy, and only where these four powers are effectively applied can we say that there is thoroughgoing, direct, popular sovereignty. Before there was any complete democracy, people elected their officials and representatives and then could not hold them responsible. This was only indirect democracy or a representative system of government. The people could not control the government directly but only through their representatives. For direct control of the government it is necessary that the people practice these four forms of popular sovereignty. Only then can we speak of government by all the people. This means that our four hundred millions shall be king, exerting their kingly authority and controlling the great affairs of state by means of the four powers of the people. These four powers are also called political powers and are powers for control of the government.

The government's own power to transact business may be called the power to work, to work on behalf of the people. If the people are very powerful, whether the government can work or not and what kind of work it does will depend entirely upon the will of the people. If the government is very powerful, as soon as it starts work it can display great strength, and whenever the people want it to stop, it will have to stop. In a nutshell, if the people are really to have direct control over the power of government they must be able to command at any time the actions of the government.

With the people exerting these four great powers to control the government, what methods will the government use in performing its work? In order that the government may have a complete organ through which to do its best work, there must be a quintuple-power constitution. A government is not complete and cannot do its best work for the people unless it is based upon a quintuple-power constitution. I spoke before of an American scholar who advanced the new theory that what a nation fears most is an all-powerful, uncontrollable government, yet what it most desires is an all-powerful government which the people can use and which will seek the people's welfare. Popular rule cannot really prevail until there is the latter kind of government. We are now making a distinction between sovereignty and ability; we are saying that the people are like the engineer and the government like the machinery. On the one hand, we want government machinery to be all-powerful so that it can do any sort of work; on the other hand, we want the engineer-people to be very strong so that they can control the all-powerful machinery. Now what great powers are the people and the government each to have in order that they may balance each other? I have already discussed the four powers on the people's side—suffrage, recall, initiative, and referendum. On the side of the government there must be five powers—executive, legislative, judicial, civil service examination, and censoring. When the four political powers of the people control the five governing powers of the government, then we will have a completely democratic government organ, and the strength of the people and of the government will be well balanced. This diagram will help us to understand more clearly the relation between these powers:

POLITICAL POWER OF THE PEOPLE

Suffrage Recall Initiative Referendum

ADMINISTRATIVE POWER OF THE GOVERNMENT

Legislature Judiciary Executive Civil Service Examinations Censorship

The political power above is in the hands of the people, the administrative power below is in the hands of the government. The people control the government through the suffrage, the recall, the initiative, and the referendum; the government works for the people through its legislative, judicial, executive, civil examination, and censoring departments. With these nine powers in operation and preserving a balance, the problem of democracy will truly be solved and tbe government will have a definite course to follow. The materials for this new plan have been discovered before now. Switzerland has already applied three of the political powers but does not have the recall. Some of the northwestern states in the United States have taken over the three political rights from Switzerland and have added the right of recall. Suffrage is the people's power most widely exercised in the world to-day. Switzerland is already exercising three of the popular powers and one fourth of the United States is exercising all four. Where the four powers have been exercised in a careful, compact way the results have been excellent. They are facts of experience, not mere hypothetical ideals. We will be safe in using these methods and will not run into any danger.

All governmental powers were formerly monopolized by kings and emperors, but after the revolutions they were divided into three groups: thus the United States, after securing its independence, established a government with three coordinate departments, with splendid results. Other nations followed the example of the United States. But foreign governments have never exercised more than these three powers—legislative, executive, and judicial. What is the source of the two new features in our quintuple-power constitution? They come from old China. China long ago had the independent systems of civil service examination and censorship and they were very effective. The imperial censors or historiographers of the Manchu dynasty and the official advisers of the T'ang dynasty made a fine censoring system. The power of censorship includes the power to impeach, which other governments have but which is placed in the legislative body and is not a separate governmental power. The selection of real talent and ability through examinations has been characteristic of China for thousands of years. Modern foreign scholars who have studied Chinese institutions give high praise to

China's old independent examination system, and there have been imitations of the system for the selection of able men in the West. Great Britain's civil service examinations are modeled after the old Chinese system, but only ordinary officials are examined. The British system does not yet possess the spirit of the independent examination system of old China. In Chinese political history, the three governmental powers—judicial, legislative, and executive—were vested in the emperor. The other powers of civil service examination and censorship were separate from the throne. The old autocratic government of China can also be said to have had three departments and so was very different from the autocratic governments of the West in which all power was monopolized by the king or emperor himself. During the period of autocratic government in China, the emperor still did not have sole authority over the power of examination and censorship. So China in a way had three coordinate departments of government, just as the modern democracies of the West have their three departments, with this difference—the Chinese government has exercised the powers of autocracy, censorship, and civil examination for many thousands of years, while Western governments have exercised legislative, judicial, and executive powers for only a little over a century. However, the three governmental powers in the West have been imperfectly applied and the three coordinate powers of ancient China led to many abuses. If we now want to combine the best from China and the best from other countries and guard against all kinds of abuse in the future, we must take the three Western governmental powers the executive, legislative, and judicial; add to them the old Chinese powers of examination and censorship and make a finished wall, a quintuple-power government. Such a government will be the most complete and the finest in the world, and a state with such a government will indeed be of the people, by the people, and for the people.

Each of these four popular powers and five governmental powers has its own focus and function; we must separate them clearly and not confuse them.

From the standpoint of function, the governmental powers are mechanical powers. In order to make this large machinery, which can develop tremendous horse power, function most effectively, we make it work in five directions. The popular powers are the powers of control which the people exercise directly over this high-powered machinery. The four powers of the people, we may say, are four controls which the people manipulate in order to make the machinery move and stop. The government works for the people and its five powers are five forms of work or five directions of work. The people control the government and their four powers are four methods of control. Only as the government is given such power and the opportunity to work in these different directions can it manifest great dignity and authority and become an all-powerful government. Only as the people are given great power and the various checks upon the government will they not be afraid of the government becoming all-powerful and uncontrollable. The people can then at any time command the government to move or to stop. The prestige of the government will grow and the power of the people will increase. With such an administrative power on the part of the government and such political power on the part of the people, we will be able to realize the ideal of the American scholar—an all-powerful government seeking the welfare of the people—and to blaze the way for the building of a new world.

THE PRINCIPLE OF LIVELIHOOD

LECTURE ONE

Delivered on August 3, 1924.

The subject of my lecture to-day is *Min Sheng Chu I,* the Principle of the People's Livelihood. *Min Sheng* is a worn phrase in China. We talk about *Kuo Chi Min Sheng,* national welfare and the people's livelihood, but I fear that we pay only lip service to these words and have not really sought to understand them. I cannot see that they have held much meaning for us. But if, in this day of scientific knowledge, we will bring the phrase into the realm of scientific discussion and study its social and economic implications, we shall find that it takes on an immeasurable significance. I propose to-day a definition for *Min Sheng,* the People's livelihood. It denotes the livelihood of the people,—the existence of society, the welfare of the nation, the life of the masses. And now I shall use the phrase *Min Sheng* to describe one of the greatest problems that has emerged in the West during the past century or more, and that is social problem.

The problem of livelihood is now rising like a tide in every country. Yet the problem is comparatively new, with a history of not much over a century. What has caused the sudden emergence of this question in the last hundred years? Briefly, the rapid progress of material civilization all over the world, the great development of industry and the sudden increase in the productive power of the human race. Candidly speaking, the problem arose with the invention of machinery and with the gradual substitution of natural power for human labor in the most civilized nations. The natural forces of steam, heat, water and electricity began to be used in place of human strength, and copper and iron in place of human bone and sinew. Since the invention of machinery, one man in charge of one machine has been able to do the work of one hundred or one thousand men. A great discrepancy has arisen between the productive power of the machine and human productive power. The most diligent worker can hardly do more than two or three men's work in one day and can never do more than ten men's work, which means that a most diligent man with the most powerful physique and the greatest strength and energy could not possibly produce more goods than ten ordinary men could. There is not much difference in the productive strength of ordinary men, but there is a vast difference between the productiveness of a machine and the productiveness of simple human labor. When human labor alone is employed, the most powerful and industrious workers cannot accomplish more than ten times the amount of the ordinary worker, but when machinery is employed, the most lazy and common worker in charge of it can accomplish hundreds, thousands of times as much as the best worker without machinery. Productiveness is now a very different thing from what it was a few decades ago before the introduction of machinery.

Since the invention of machinery, therefore, the world has undergone a revolution in production. Machinery has usurped the place of human labor, and men who possessed machinery have taken wealth away from those who did not have machinery. Following the introduction of machinery, great numbers of men suddenly lost their occupations and were unable to get work or to obtain food. Westerners have called this great change the Industrial Revolution. On account of this revolution the workers suffered greatly. This is why, during the last few decades, a social problem has come into existence, the result of an effort to relieve this kind of suffering.

It is this social problem that I am discussing to-day in the Principle of Livelihood. Why not follow the West and speak directly of socialism? Why use the old Chinese term *Min Shèng* in its stead? There is a very significant reason for this which we shall consider. Since its first development, and especially since the Industrial Revolution, machinery has become a serious social problem and has stimulated the rise of socialistic theories. But although socialism has been a growing force for several decades, Western nations have not yet found a solution for the questions involved in it, and a severe dispute is still raging over them.

Is the Principle of Livelihood really different from socialism? Socialism deals primarily with the economic problems of society; that is, the common problem of a living. Since the introduction of machinery, a large number of people have had their work taken away from them and workers generally have been unable to maintain their existence. Socialism arose as an effort to solve the living problem, and from this standpoint, the social question is also the economic question, and the principle of livelihood is the main theme of socialism. But now every country's socialism has different theories and different proposals for social reconstruction. Scholars have divided socialists into two groups: Utopian socialists, whose ideal is similar to Lieh-tze's* dream of the *Land of the Hwa-hsu* people; and the scientific socialists, who use only scientific methods in the study of social problems. The Utopian socialists would reform society and make a peaceful and happy state simply out of their imagination. Scientific socialists advocated the use of scientific methods in solving social problems. In this epoch, when material civilization is advancing so rapidly and science is becoming so powerful, all study must be based upon scientific principles in order to achieve satisfactory results, and we cannot expect a solution of the social question until careful scientific research has been made.

Marx worked out the theory that all human activity upon the globe which has been preserved in written records for succeeding generations can be called history; and all human

* A Chinese philosopher of the fifth century before Christ.

history, viewed in this way, gravitates about material forces. This latter point was the new emphasis which Marx gave to history. If the material basis of life changes, the world also changes; human behavior, moreover, is determined by the material environment, and so the history of human civilization is the story of adaptation to material environment.

What about the economic theory of history enunciated by Marx? In 1848 Marx's disciples held a world congress of socialists at Brussels and decided upon several policies which are still adhered to by large numbers of Marxian socialists everywhere. After the European War broke out, Russia began to put Marx's theories into practice, but of late she has made great changes in the interpretation of his theories. After the European War the disciples of Marx all began to quarrel over matters of theory. The socialist parties of Germany, France and Russia had formerly been common followers of Marx and had been branches of the Internationale, but after the differences of opinion arose, they began to attack and to vilify each other and to accuse each other of disloyalty to Marxism. As a result of the attacks of this branch upon that and of this National Socialist Party upon that, Marx's theories began to be seriously questioned.

Have material forces really been the center of gravity in history? Marx discovered that history gravitated about material forces; was his principle correct or not? After a few years of experiment with it following the European War, many people are saying that the principle is wrong. What, then, is the central force in history? Our Kuomintang has been advocating the Principle of Livelihood for over twenty years now; we have not championed socialism but the *Min Sheng* Principle. Are the spheres of these two doctrines in any way related? Recently an American disciple of Marx, named Williams,* after making a deep study of Marx's philosophy, came to the con-

* Referring to Maurice Williams, author of "Social Interpretation of History."

clusion that the disagreement between fellow socialists is due to defects in the Marxism doctrines. He sets forth the view that the materialistic conception of history is wrong; that the social problem, not material forces, is the center which determines the course of history, and that subsistence is the heart of the social problem. This social interpretation of history he believes is the only reasonable one. The problem of livelihood is the problem of subsistence. The new theory of this American scholar tallies exactly with the third principle of our party. Williams' theory means that livelihood is the central force in social progress, and that social progress is the central force in history; hence the struggle for a living and not material forces determines history. We have held forth the Pinciple of Livelihood for twenty years; when we first studied and pondered upon this question, we felt that the term *Min Sheng* defined the field of social problems better than the terms "socialism" or "communism," so we chose to use it. We little foresaw at that time how the clarifying of principles and development of knowledge following a European war would lead students of the Marx school to discover the same point. This shows that our *Min Sheng* Pirnciple is consistent with the law of progress and is not a mere parroting of what contemporary scholars are saying.

According to this American scholar, the energies of mankind, both in ancient and modern times, have been spent largely in trying to solve the problem of subsistence. The struggle for existence is one of the laws of social progress and is the central force in history. Marx's materialistic theory did not set forth any law of social progress and cannot be a determining factor in history. If we want to understand clearly the positions of these two social philosophers and to know which one is right, we must make a detailed study of their doctrines and see whether these doctrines harmonize with the facts of modern social progress. Marx, in his investigation of the social problem, emphasized the material side. In dealing with material forces you inevitably come first to the question of production. Where there is no overproduction, there would naturally be no industrial revolution, and so production holds a place of prime importance in modern economics. If you want to understand modern economic conditions, you must know the facts about production. The large-scale production in modern times is made possible by labor and machinery, by the cooperation of capital and machinery together with the employment of labor. The benefits of this large-scale production are reaped largely by the capitalists themselves; the workers enjoy but a small fraction of the benefits. Consequently, the interests of capitalists and of workers are constantly clashing and when no solution of the difficulty is found, a class war breaks out. Marx held the view that class war was not something which had only followed the industrial revolution; all past history is a story of class struggle

—between masters and slaves, between landlords and serfs, between nobles and common people; in a word, between all kinds of oppressors and oppressed. Only when the social revolution was completely successful, would these warring classes be no more. It is evident from this that Marx considered class war essential to social progress, the driving force, in fact, of social progress. He made class war the cause and social progress the effect. Let us look at recent facts in the development of society to see whether this principle of cause and effect is really a law of social progress. Society has made tremendous progress in the last few decades and the details of this social progress would make a complicated story. The facts on the economic side alone cannot be described in a few words. But to summarize briefly: recent economic progress in the West may be said to have taken four forms—social and industrial reform, public ownership of transportation and communications, direct taxation, and socialized distribution. These four socionomic practices have all evolved through the method of reform, and we should see more reforms and increasing improvements as time goes on.

I shall explain these four practices a little more in detail. The first one—socionomic reform—means the use of government power to better the workingman's education and to protect his health, to improve factories and machinery so that working conditions may be perfectly safe and comfortable. Such reforms give the worker more strength for his work and make him quite willing to work; they also greatly increase the rate of production. Germany was the first country to put these socially progressive policies into operation and she obtained the best results; in recent years Great Britain and the United States have imitated her with equally good results.

The second new practice means putting electric and steam railways, steamship lines, and all the big business of the postal and telegraph service entirely under government management. When the government's great power is employed in the directon of all these great enterprises, rapid transport and convenient communication are assured. Then materials can be moved easily from all parts of the country to the factories and manufactured articles from the factories can be easily distributed to the markets for sale, without loss of time and the stoppage in transit which causes so much damage to both raw materials and manufactured goods. If private individuals, rather than the government, are intrusted with these enterprises, they either do not have enough financial resources to carry on the enterprise or they develop, through monopoly, too much obstructive power. Transportation is then certain to slow down and communications become less effective. All economic activities throughout the country suffer intangible and serious losses. Germany was the first nation to see the advantages and the disadvantages of private business and long ago put all her means of transportation and communication under the direct management of the state. During the European War, all the private transport and communication companies in the United States were brought under government direction.

The third feature of modern economic reform, direct taxation, is also a very recent development in the socio-economic method. It is applied by means of a graduated tax scale which levies a heavy income tax and inheritance tax upon capitalists and secures financial resources for the state directly from capitalists. Because of the large income of capitalists, direct taxation by the state "gets much without seeming oppressive." The old system of taxation depended entirely upon the tax on money and grain and upon the customs tariff. These methods laid the burden of national income entirely upon the poor people and let the capitalists enjoy all the privileges of the state without shouldering any financial responsibility, which was exceedingly unjust. Germany and Great Britain long ago became aware of this injustice and put into effect a plan of direct taxation.

The fourth new economic activity, socialized distribution, is a most recent development in Western society. Since the invention of money and the development of the trade system all commodities for ordinary consumption have been bought indirectly through tradesmen or merchants. The merchant buys the commodities at the lowest possible price from the producer and then sells them to the consumer; by this one transaction he earns a large commission. Such a system of distribution may be called the trade system or merchant distribution. Under such a system of distribution the consumer unconsciously suffers heavy losses. Recent studies have shown that the trade system can be improved upon, that goods do not have to be distributed by merchants but can be distributed through social organizations or by the government. The principle in this new system is that of socialized distribution, or socialism applied to distribution.

These four forms of social and ecomomic development social and economic reform, public ownership of transportation and communications, direct taxation and socialized distribution-are overthrowing old systems and giving rise to new systems. It is the constant emergence of new systems that makes constant progress possible.

What is the cause of social evolution? Why does society have to undergo these transformations? Judging by Marx's theory, we would have to say that social change is caused by class struggle and class struggle is caused by the capitalists oppression of workers. Since the interests of capitalists and workers inevitably conflict and cannot be reconciled, struggle ensues and this struggle within society is what makes for progress. Look, however, at the actual facts of social progress in the West during the last few decades. Best of all has been the development of socialized distribution which destroys the monopoly of the tradesman. Heavier taxes upon the incomes and the inheritances of the capitalists increases the wealth of the state and enables the state to take over means of transportation and communication, to improve the education and the health of workers and equipment within the factories, and to increase the productiveness of society. When production is large and products are rich, the capitalists naturally make fortunes and the workers receive high wages. From this point of view, when the capitalists improve the living conditions of the workers and increase their productivity, the workers can produce more for the capitalists. On the capitalists' side, this means greater production ; on the workers' side, higher wages. Here is a reconciliation of the interests of capitalists and workers, rather than a conflict between them. Society progresses, then, through the adjustment of major economic interests rather than through the clash of interests. If most of the economic interests of society can be harmonized, the majority of people will benefit and society will progress. The reason why we want to make these adjustments is simply because of the living problem. From ancient times until now man has exerted his energies in order to maintain his existence. And mankind's struggle for continuous existence has been the reason for society's unceasing development, the law of social progress. Class war is not the cause of social progress, it is a disease developed in the course of social progress. The cause of the disease is the inability to subsist, and the result of the disease is war. What Marx gained through his studies of social problems was a knowledge of diseases in the course of social progress. Therefore, Marx can only be called a social pathologist; we cannot say that he is a social physiologist.

According to Marx's theory of class struggle, the "surplus value" which the capitalist enjoys is taken entirely out of the workingman's labor. Marx gave all the credit for production to the labor of the industrial worker and overlooked the labor of other useful social factors. When we think about the raw material of yarn and cloth, our minds turn to cotton; when we think about the source of the cotton, our minds turn to questions of agriculture. If we want to discuss in detail the cultivation of cotton, we shall have to refer to the scientific agriculturalists who study the selection of good cotton seed and the best methods of planting and raising cotton. Many implements and machines must be used to plow the soil before the planting of the seed and to weed the soil after the planting; fertilizers must be applied to nourish the plants. When we consider the machines and the fertilizers, we have to give credit to the discoverers and manufacturers of these things. After the cotton is picked, it must be transported to the mills to be spun and woven; after the yarn and piece goods are manufactured, they must be transported to the markets for sale. This leads our minds naturally to steamships and trains and if we think why they are able to transport goods, we shall have to give credit to the inventors of steam and electric engines; if we think about the materials of which they are made, we shall have to give credit to miners and manufacturers of metals and to foresters and lumbermen. If, after the manufacture of the thread and the cloth is complete no classes in society except industrial workers use the thread or wear the cloth, these things will not have a wide market; and then, how can the capitalists make large profits and create a large surplus value? When you put these facts before you, to whom do you think the surplus value belongs? How can the workers in the factories say that it is created entirely by their own labor? The circumstances under which the surplus value is created is the same in all industries: it is the fruit not only of labor within the factories but of many useful and powerful factors in society working directly or indirectly and making a large or a small contribution towards the production or consumption of the manufactured commodities. These useful and powerful factors occupy a large place in society.

As for the industrial workers, even in such an industrially prosperous nation like the United States, they do not number more than twenty millions, one fifth of the total population; while in other countries, such as China, they represent a very small proportion of the people. If we look at the question from this standpoint, then if there is a lack of adjustment of economic interests in a highly industralized nation, leading to conflict and war, we shall not see one working class in a struggle against one capitalist class but most of the useful and able factors in all society lined up against the capitalists. And it is because these numerous social factors want to find a living and to eliminate economic strife that they are introducing public distribution of goods, heavy taxes upon capitalist incomes and inheritances for the development of national transportation and communication, reform of living conditions among workers and of working conditions in the factories, and all sorts of practices which will help to harmonize the larger number of economic interests within the nation. Since these various methods of economic adjustment have developed in the West, society has made much progress and the majority of the people have come to enjoy happiness. Marx, in his study of social problems, found only one of the diseases of society; he did not discover the law of social progress and the central force in history. As stated by the American scholar, the struggle for subsistence is the law of social progress and is the central force of history. The struggle for existence is the same thing as the problem of livelihood, and therefore the problem of livelihood can be said to be the driving force in social progress. When we fully understand this principle, it will be easy for us to find another solution for the social problem.

Marx's assumption that class struggle is a cause of social progress puts effect before cause. Because of this confusion in source ideas, Marx's theory has not been borne out and has sometimes been directly contradicted by subsequent facts in social history. For instance, Marx's disciples in 1848 held an international congress of communists and made various declarations. The International Communist League organized at this time was dissolved at the time of the Franco-Prussian War. Later, the Second International was organized, differing from the First International in several particulars. The First International stood wholly upon the theory of class struggle, advocated revolutionary methods for the reconstruction of society and no compromise with the capitalists; the latter is known as absolute nonco-operation. Political activity of members in the national assemblies was forbidden by the party as an unscientific method. But later the German Communists all began to agitate in the Reichstag, while in Great Britain the Labor Party has recently under a constitutional monarchy, been able to organize a cabinet. These facts indicate that many of the political and economic changes which have occurred have not followed the procedure outlined by the First International. The wide difference in policy between the First and the Second International aggravated the strife among the disciples of Marx, a thing unlooked for by Marx in his day. Truly, as my theory states, action is easy but understanding difficult. Marx wanted to use science in the solution of the social problem. He came, as the result of his research, to the conclusion that the capitalist system would certainly collapse in the future; as capitalism flourished, competition within the system would become severer, the larger capitalists would be sure to swallow up the smaller capitalists, and finally only two classes would be left in society—the extremely wealthy capitalists and the extremely poor workers. When capitalism had reached its peak, it would break up rapidly of its own accord and a capitalist state would follow. Then socialism in the course of nature would come into force and a free socialist state would be established. In

Marx's judgment, the highly capitalistic states had already reached the period of dissolution, and so a revolution would rise immediately. But the facts of Western history, in the seventy-odd years since Marx, have directly contradicted his theory.

As to the matter of working hours, Marx thought that the eight-hour day would diminish productiveness. But when Germany put the shorter working-day into effect, productiveness was increased and exceeded that in other countries. Great Britain and the United States were amazed. They had thought that reduction in working hours and greater expenditure for protection of workmen would decrease production; how, then, had Germany increased production by these policies? Their amazement led them to study conditions in Germany, and later, when they undertstood the new economic principles they began to imitate Germany's methods. Marx in his day did not see these principles, so he came to a false conclusion.

Again, according to Marx's researches, if the capitalists want a larger surplus value, they must fulfill three conditions—reduce wages, lengthen the working-day, and raise the price of the manufactured product. That these three conditions are illogical we can prove from the greatest money-making industry of modern times. You have all heard of the Ford factories in the United States. The factories are immense, and their enormous output of motor cars is distributed all over the world. The profits from these factories run above several score millions of dollars.

Now let us compare the industrial and economic principles which these great money-making automobile factories maintain with Marx's theory of surplus value. Marx's three essential conditions for increasing surplus value are flatly contradicted. Marx said that the capitalist would have to lengthen the working-day; the Ford factories have shortened the working-day. Marx said that the capitalist would have to reduce wages; the Ford factories have raised wages. Marx said the capitalist have to raise the price of the manufactured product; the Ford factories have reduced the price of their product. Marx did not foresee these contradictions, so his conclusion was seriously and peculiarly false. All that Marx knew from his long study of social problems was facts in past history; he did not at all anticipate what would happen in the future. Consequently, his disciples are wanting to make changes in his theories. The fundamental aim of Marx's social philosophy was the overthrow of capitalists. But whether capitalists ought to be overthrown or not is an important question which we must study in detail before we can answer clearly. This shows again that it is very difficult to understand but quite easy to act.

Here is the essence of Marx's theory of surplus value. The capitalists' money is stripped from the surplus value created by labor. The capitalists' production depends upon the workers, the workers' production depends upon materials, and the buying and selling of materials depends upon merchants. In all kinds of production, the capitalists and the merchant class take all the profit and rob the worker of the money he has earned by blood and sweat. Therefore, capitalists and tradesmen are harmful to the workers and to the world and should be destroyed. But Marx's conclusion was that the capitalists would be destroyed first and then the merchant class. The world now is making steady progress and initiating new reforms daily. Take, for example, the new practice of socialized distribution, also called by the name of co-operative societies. These societies are organized by a union of many workers. If the workers buy the clothing and food which they need indirectly through retail merchants, the merchants will demand a profit and make a lot of money, while the workers will have to spend much more upon their purchases. In order to buy good articles at a low price the workers themselves effect an organization and open their own store to sell them what they need. In this way they can buy all goods which they ordinarily use from their own store. The supplies are handy and cheap and at the end of every year the surplus profit which the store makes is divided among the customers according to the proportion of their purchases. It is on account of this division of profits in proportion to the amount of purchase that the stores are called consumers' co-operative societies. A large number of banks and productive factories in Great Britain are now managed by these co-operative societies. The rise of these societies has eliminated a great many commercial stores. Those who once looked upon these stores as unimportant commercial shops now regard them as powerful organizations. Due to the rapid spread of such organizations the big British merchants have now all become producers. The development of these co-operative societies as a solution for the social problem is a side issue, yet it has disproved

Marx's conclusion that capitalists would be destroyed before the merchant class. This inconsistency of Marx's deductions with modern facts is another evidence that my theory—knowledge is difficult, action easy—cannot be effaced.

Again, according to Marx's theory, the great industries of the world depend upon production and production depends upon capitalists, which means that with good production and large capital industry can expand and make profits. What light do industrial conditions in China throw upon this theory? The largest industrial establishment in China is the Han-yeh-ping Company (the Hanyang Iron and Steel Works), whose large factories specialize in the manufacture of steel. If there were a grain of truth in Marx's theories, the Han-yeh-ping Company should have made profit and grown rapidly. Why, then, is it failing? If we study conditions in this one company (the Han-yeh-ping Company), we shall see that the heart of industry is a community of consumers. Industry does not depend solely upon capital in production. Although the Han-yeh-ping Company has a large amount of capital, yet the steel which it produces does not find a source of consumption in China and so cannot expand or make profit. Because industry centers about a spending society, all the great modern industries manufacture commodities according to the needs of the consumer. The more intelligent workers now are also co-operating with the consumers. What is consumption but a question of helping all the people to subsist, a question of livelihood? So industry has to rest upon the livelihood of the people.

Livelihood is the center of government, the center of economics, the center of all historical movements. Just as men once misjudged the center of the solar system, so the old socialists mistook material forces for the center of history. The confusions which have resulted may be compared to those which followed the conclusions of the old astronomers that the earth was the center of our solar system. In chronological calculations there was always an error of one month in every three years. Later, when the mistake was corrected and the sun was considered the center of the solar system, there was an error of only one day in every three years. If we want to clear away the confusions from within the social problem, we must correct this mistake in social science. We can no longer say that material issues are the central force in history. We must let the political, social, and economic movements of history gravitate about the problem of livelihood. We must recognize livelihood as the center of social history. When we have made a thorough investigation of this central problem, then we can find a way to a solution of the social problem.

LECTURE TWO

Delivered on August 10, 1924.

The Kuomintang some time ago in its party platform settled upon two methods by which the Principle of Livelihood is to be carried out. The first method is equalization of landownership and the second is regulation of capital. If we follow these two methods we can solve the livelihood problem in China. The different countries of the world, because of varying conditions and varying degrees of capitalistic development, must necessarily follow different methods in dealing with the livelihood problem. Many Chinese scholars who have been absorbing all forms of Western knowledge have thought that we could solve our problem by imitating the West, without realizing how divided are the socialist parties of the West upon social questions and how far away they still are from a single course of action. The Marxians would solve all social questions by a dictatorship of the proletariat and all political and economic problems by revolution; they are the radical group. Another group of socialists advocates peaceful methods and the use of political action and negotiation. These two factions are in constant and severe conflict in Europe and America and each has its own line of action. Russia in her Revolution employed the revolutionary method for dealing with her political and economic problems. But what we have seen in the six years following the Revolution shows that the revolutionary method was completely successful only so far as the political problem went; it cannot be said to have wholly solved the economic problem. Soviet Russia's new economic policy is still in an experimental stage, and it makes us realize that revolutionary schemes cannot entirely clear up economic difficulties. For this reason many Western scholars are opposing Russia's revolutionary plan and are advocating political action instead. As political action does not accomplish political and social reform in a day, this group is made up of the believers in slow progress, negotiation and peaceable means. They do not think that the highly capitalistic states of the West should utilize Marx's method and attempt a precipitate solution of the social problem; they think that only peaceful methods will fully settle the problem.

These peaceful methods are the four which I described in my last lecture—social and economic reform, nationalization of transportation and communications, direct taxation or the income tax, and socialized distribution or cooperative societies. They are quite different from the methods which Marx proposed, and if we follow them as the way to economic reconstruction, we will be in opposition to Marx's revolutionary schemes. Various Western nations are putting one after another of these four plans into operation, and although the results so far are not all that they hope for, yet they feel that the ultimate solution of the social problem does lie in these four plans, and many socialists are supporting them. At the same time that they indorse these peaceful methods, they resist Marx's revolutionary methods.

When Russia first started the Revolution, she was hoping to settle the social question; the political question was secondary. The Revolution resulted, however, in a solution of the political question but no solution of the social question, exactly opposite to that which was anticipated.

The Principle of Livelihood which the Kuomintang advocates is not merely a high ideal; it is also a driving force in society, it is the center of all historical movements. Only as this principle is applied can our social problems be solved, and only as our social problems are solved can mankind enjoy the greatest blessings.

What methods should our Kuomintang employ for the solution of the livelihood problem, in view of the position China occupies and the times in which we are living? We must base our methods not upon abstruse theories or upon empty learning, but upon facts, and not facts peculiar to foreign countries but facts observable in China. Only when we have facts data can we settle upon methods of procedure Method based simply upon theory will not be trustworthy, because theories may be true or false, and they must be verified by experiment. A newly proposed scientific theory must produce facts; it must work out in practice, before we can say it is true. In working for a solution of our social problems, we must, therefore, ground ourselves upon facts and not trust to mere theories. What are these basic facts in China? All of us have a share in the distressing poverty of the Chinese people. There is no especially rich class, there is only a general poverty. The "inequalities between rich and poor" which the Chinese speak of are only differences within the poor class, differences in degree of poverty. As a matter of fact, the great capitalists of China, in comparison with the great foreign capitalists, are really poor; the rest of the poor people are extremely poor. Since China's largest capitalists are poor men out in the world, then all the Chinese people must be counted as poor. There are no great rich among us, only differences between the fairly poor and the extremely poor. How can we equalize this condition so that there will be no more extreme poverty?

The process of social change and capitalistic development usually begins with the landowners, and from the landowners goes on to the merchant, and finally to the capitalist. Landowners arose out of the feudal system. Europe is not yet completely free from the feudal system, but China destroyed her feudal system as long ago as the Ch'in dynasty.* When the feudal system was in existence, the nobles who owned land were the rich, and the people without land were the poor. Although China broke away from the

* 246–207 B.C.

feudal system two thousand years ago, yet because of the lack of industrial and commercial progress, social conditions now are just about what they were at that time. Since the currents of Western economic life have begun to rush into China, all of our old systems have undergone a process of change. The land question has felt the first and most serious effects of the modern Western impact. But this marked effect of economic development upon land values is true not only in China; all other countries have experienced the same thing. At first they did not notice the fact or pay much attention to it. Not until the disturbances in the economic order became acute did they give their attention, and then it was not easy to remedy the situation, "to turn back with accumulated burden". The Kuomintang must, as a matter of foresight and of precaution against future difficulties, find a solution of this problem of fluctuation in land values.

Western books on socialism are full of interesting stories about rise in land values. There was a place in Australia, for instance, where land was very cheap before the building up of a trade center. The government once wanted to sell at auction a piece of land which at the time was simply waste ground, covered with trash piles and of no other use. Nobody was willing to pay a high price for the land. Suddenly a drunken fellow broke into the place where the auctioning was going on. The auctioneer was just then calling for bids on the land; there had been bids of one hundred, two hundred, two hundred and fifty dollars. As no one would bid higher, the auctioneer then called, "Who will bid three hundred?" At that moment the drunken fellow, now completely befuddled, yelled out, "I will give three hundred!" The auctioneer then took down his name and assigned him the land. Since the land was sold, the crowd left and the drunken man also walked away. The next day, the auctioneer sent the man a bill for the price of the land, but the man did not remember what he had done in his drunken condition the day before and would not acknowledge the bill against him. When he finally did call to mind what he had done, he was bitterly regretful; but since it was impossible to default to the government, he had to try all sorts of plans and exhaust all his resources in order to pay over the three hundred dollars to the auctioneer. For a long time after he aquired the land, he was not able to give it any attention. Over a decade passed; tall buildings and great mansions had been erected all around that piece of land, and the price of land had soared. Some people offered the owner of the empty tract millions of dollars, but he refused to let it go. He simply rented out his land and took the rent money. Finally, when the land was worth tens of millions, the old drunkard became the wealthiest man in Australia. All this wealth came from that first investment in a three-hundred-dollar lot. The owner of the land was of course delighted when he became a millionaire, but what about other people? After paying three hundred dollars for the land, the man did not do a bit of work to improve it; in fact he let it alone. While he slept or sat with folded hands enjoying his success, the millions poured into his lap.

To whom did these millions really belong? In my opinion, they belonged to everybody. For it was because the people in the community chose this section as an industrial and commercial center and made improvements upon it, that this tract of land increased in value and gradually reached such a high price. So foreign scholars speak of the profits which the landowner gets out of the increased price of land as "unearned increment," a very different thing from the profits which industrial and commercial manufacturers get by dint of hard mental and physical labor, by buying cheap and selling dear, by all sorts of business schemes and methods. We have already felt that the profits which the industrial and commercial leaders make by monopolies over materials are not just profits. But these men at least work hard; the landowner, however, simply holds what he has, does not use a bit of mental effort, and reaps huge profits. Yet, what is it that makes the value of his land rise? The improvements which people make around his land and the competition which they carry on for possession of his land. When the price of land rises, every single commodity in the community also rises in price. So we may truly say that the money which the people in the community earn through their business is indirectly and imperceptibly robbed from them by the landowner.

But what really is the Principle of Livelihood? In my last lecture I revealed a little of what it means; I said that *Min Sheng,* or Livelihood, has been the central force in the cultural progress of society, in the improvement of economic organization, and in moral evolution. Livelihood is the driving power in all social movements; and if livelihood does not go right, social culture cannot advance, economic organization cannot improve, morals will decline, and many injustices such as class war, cruelty to workers, and other forms of oppression will spring up—all because of the failure to remedy the unfortunate conditions of livelihood. All social changes are effects; the search for livelihood is the cause.

The first effect of the recent Western economic invasion of China has been upon land. Many people have taken land as something to gamble with and have gone into land speculation or "land squabbling," as the common saying puts it. Much land which would not be worth a great deal until ten or twenty years later, and which would not naturally have been highly valued, has been raised in price ahead of time through the wire pulling of speculators. This makes the rise in land values all the more uneven.

Western nations have not yet found any satisfactory methods to deal with these evil practices arising out of the land question. If we want to solve the land question we must do it now; if we wait until industry and commerce are fully developed, we will have no way to solve it. Now that Western influences are coming in and our industry and commerce are undergoing such marked transformations, inequalities are arising not only between the rich and the poor, but also between common owners of land. The aim of our party's *Min Sheng* Principle is to equalize the financial resources in society. Our first step is to be the solution of the land problem.

The methods for the solution of the land problem are different in various countries, and each country has its own peculiar difficulties. The plan which we are following is simple and easy—the equalization of landownership. If our landowners were like the great landowners of Europe and had developed tremendous power, it would be exceedingly difficult for us to solve the land question. But China does not have such big landowners, and the power of the small landowners is still rather weak. If we attack the problem now, we can solve it; but we lose the present opportunity, we can never find a way out. The discussion of the land problem naturally causes a feeling of fear among the landowners, but if the Kuomintang policy is followed, present landowners can set their hearts at rest.

What is our policy? We propose that the government shall buy back the land, if necessary, according to the amount of land tax and the price of the land. How indeed, can the price of the land be determined? I would advocate that the landowner himself should fix the price. The landowner reports the value of his land to the government and the government levies a land tax accordingly. Many people think that if the landowners make their own assessment, they will undervalue the land and the government will lose out. For instance, the landowner might report a piece of land worth a hundred thousand dollars as worth only ten thousand. According to an assessment of a hundred thousand dollars the government would receive a thousand dollars in taxes, but according to an assessment of ten thousand, the government would get only one hundred dollars. The tax office would of course lose nine hundred dollars. But suppose the government makes two regulation: first, that it will collect taxes according to the declared value of the land; second, that it can also buy back the land at the same price. The landowner who assesses his hundred-thousand-dollar land at ten thousand dollars fools the government out of nine hundred dollars and naturally gets the best of the bargain; but if the government buys back his land at the price of ten thousand dollars, he loses nine thousand dollars, a tremendous loss. According to my plan, if the landowner makes a low assessment, he will be afraid lest the government buy back his land at that value and make him lose his property; if he makes too high an assessment, he will be afraid of the government taxes according to this value and his loss through heavy taxes. Comparing these two serious possibilities, he will certainly not want to report the value of his land too high or too low; he will strike a mean and report the true market price to the government. As a result, neither landowner nor government will suffer.

After the land values have been fixed, we should have a regulation by law that from that year on, all increase in land values, which in other countries means heavier taxation, shall revert to the community. This is because the increase in land values is due to improvement made by society and to the progress of industry and commerce. China's industry and commerce have made little progress for thousands of years, so land values have scarcely changed through all these generations. But as soon as there is progress and improvement, as in the modern cities of China, land prices change every day, sometimes increasing a thousandfold or ten thousandfold. The credit for the improvement and progress belongs to the energy and business activity of all the people and not merely to a few private individuals. For example: if a landowner now assesses his land at ten thousand dollars and several decades later that land rises in value to a million dollars, this increase of nine hundred and ninety thousand dollars would, in our plan, become a public fund as a reward to all those who had improved the community and who had advanced industry and commerce around the land. This proposal that all future increment shall be given to the community is the "equalization of land ownership" advocated by the Kuomintang; it is the *Min Sheng* Principle. When the landowners clearly understand the principle involved in our plan for equalization of landownership, they will not be apprehensive. Our plan provides that land now fixed in value shall still be privately owned. If the land problem can be solved, one half of the problem of livelihood will be solved.

When modern, enlightened cities levy land taxes, the burdens upon the common people are lightened and many other advantages follow. Although land values in foreign countries have risen very high and the landowners are consequently enjoying large incomes, yet the advance of science and the development of machinery, together with the heavy production on the part of machine-owning capitalists, have made the immense incomes which capitalists enjoy a far more serious matter than landowners' incomes. The capitalists in China with the largest incomes are still landowners, not machine owners. So it should be very easy for us now to equalize land ownership, to regulate capital, and to find a way out of the land problem.

Speaking of taxing or buying back land according to its value, we must make clear one important point. Land value refers only to the value of the bare land; it does not include improvements made by human labor or construction work upon the surface. For instance, if land valued at ten thousand dollars has upon it buildings valued at a million dollars, the land tax at the rate of one percent would be only one hundred dollars. But if the land were bought back by the government, compensation would have to be made for the million dollars' worth of buildings upon the land. Other land with artificial improvements such as trees, embankments, drains, and such would have to be paid for in the same way.

If we want to solve the livelihood problem in China and "by one supreme effort win eternal ease," it will not be enough to depend upon the regulation of capital. The income tax levied in foreign countries is one method of regulating capital. But have these other countries solved the livelihood problem? China cannot be compared to foreign countries; it is not sufficient for us to regulate capital. Other countries are rich while China is poor; other countries have a surplus of production while China is not producing enough. So China must not only regulate private capital, but she must also develop state capital and promote industry. First, we must begin to build means of communication, railroads and waterways, on a large scale. Second, we must open up mines. China is rich in minerals, but alas, they are buried in the earth! Third, we must hasten to foster manufacturing. Although China has a multitude of workers, yet she has no machinery and so cannot compete with other nations. Goods used throughout China depend upon other countries for manufacture and transportation hither, and consequently our economic rights and interests are simply leaking away. If we want to recover these rights and interests, we must quickly employ state power to promote industry, use machinery in production, and give employment to the workers of the whole nation. When all the workers have employment and can use machinery in production, then China will have a great, new source of wealth. If we do not use state power to build up these enterprises but leave them in the hands of private Chinese or of foreign business men, the result will be simply the expansion of private capital and the emergence of a great wealthy class with the consequent inequalities in society. So in working out our Principle of Livelihood, we cannot use or apply in China the methods of Marx. The reason for this is obvious. Russia has been trying to apply Marx's methods since the Revolution until now, yet she wants to change to a new economic policy, because the economic life of her society has not reached the standard of economic life in Great Britain or the United States, and is not ripe for the application of Marx's methods. If Russia's economic standards are below those of Great Britain or the United States, how could China's economic standards possibly be high enough for the application of Marx's methods? Even Marx's disciples say that we cannot use his methods for the solution of all social problems in China.

The youthful scholars to-day who are pinning their faith on Marxism, and who, as soon as socialism is mentioned, advocate Marx's way for the solution of China's social and economic problems. But they fail to realize that China now is suffering from poverty, not from unequal distribution of wealth. In seeking a solution for our livelihood problem, we are not going to propose some impracticable and radical method and then wait until industry is developed. We want a plan which will anticipate dangers and forearm us against emergencies, which will check the growth of large private capital and prevent the social disease of extreme inequality between the rich and the poor. Such a plan will rightly solve our immediate social problems and will not be like first wearing furs and then hoping for the north winds.

As I said a little while ago, the regulations of capital to-day in China will not be enough to solve our livelihood problem. It will also be necessary to build up state capital. What does this mean? Simply the development of state industries. The details of this scheme can be found in the second volume of my *Plans for National Reconstruction,** under the heading "Material econstruction or Industrial

* Written in 1918. In three parts : Psychological Reconstruction, Material Reconstruction, Social Reconstruction.

Measures." In this volume I have given the outline of the plan for building up state capital. As I said before, money was capital in the commercial age, but machinery is capital in the industrial age. The state should lead in business enterprises and set up all kinds of productive machinery which will be the property of the state. During the European War, it was the policy of each country to nationalize its great industries and its factories. But this policy was abandoned soon afterwards. China has never had any great capitalists; if the state can control and develop capital and give the benefits to all the people, it will be easy to avoid the conflicts with capitalists. The United States has developed capital in three ways: through railroads, through manufacturing, and through mining. We shall not be able to promote one of these three great industries by our own knowledge and experience with our own capital; we cannot but depend upon the already created capital of other countries. If we wait until we ourselves have enough capital before we start to promote industry, the process of development will be exceedingly slow. China now has no machinery to speak of. We have only six or seven thousand miles of railroad. To meet our needs, we should have mileage ten times as great. At least sixty or seventy thousand miles are necessary. So we shall certainly have to borrow foreign capital to develop our communication and transportation facilities, and foreign brains and experience to manage them.

As for our mines, we have not even begun to open them. China exceeds the United States in population and in size of territory, yet the United States produces 600,000,000 tons of coal and 90,000,000 tons of steel every year, while China does not produce a thousandth of that amount. If we want to open up our mines quickly, again we must borrow foreign capital. To construct steamships, to develop a merchant marine, and to build up all kinds of manufacturing industries on a large scale, it will be absolutely necessary for us to borrow foreign capital. If these three great industries—communications, mining, and manufacturing—should all begin to thrive in China, our annual income from them would be very great. If the industries are carried on by the state, the rights and privileges which they bring will be enjoyed by all the people. The people of the whole nation will then have a share in the profits of capital and will not be injured by capital. In the solution of the social problem, we have the same object in view as that in foreign countries: to make everybody contented and happy, free from the suffering caused by the unequal distribution of wealth and property.

Our Three Principles of the People mean government "of the people, by the people, and for the people"—that is, a state belonging to all the people, a government controlled by all the people, and rights and benefits for the enjoyment of all the people. If this is true, the people will have a share in everything. When the people share everything in the state, then will we truly reach the goal of the *Min Sheng* Principle, which is Confucius' hope of a "great commonwealth."

LECTURE THREE

Delivered on August 17, 1924

My topic to-day is the "food problem." When you hear this, you will say that eating food is a daily and familiar habit. People often remark that nothing in the world is easier than eating. It is true that eating is a very simple and customary activity; why, then, should there be any problem connected with it? We do not realize that food is a most vital problem of livelihood which, if not solved, will cause the whole problem of livelihood to fail of solution. The chief problem in the *Min Sheng Principle* is the food problem. The saying of the ancients, "The nation looks upon the people as its foundation; the people look upon food as their heaven," is revealing as to the importancce of the food question.

It is easy to solve the difficulty when one person or one family lacks food, but when a whole nation, such as China with her four hundred millions, does not have any adequate supply of food, the problem becomes very grave and difficult of solution. Is China's food supply really sufficient or not? Do the Chinese people have enough to eat? Kwangtung Province imports $70,000,000 worth of food annually. If no rice were imported for one month, Kwangtung would at once be disturbed by a food famine, which proves that Kwangtung does not have an adequate food supply. We are speaking only of Kwangtung, yet many other provinces are faced with similar conditions. There are many reasons why China does not have an adequate food supply; the main reason is the lack of progress in agricultural science and the next reason is foreign economic domination.

When we speak of the Principle of Livelihood we mean that we want our four hundred millions all to have food and very cheap food;

only when there is abundant, cheap food can we say that livelihood problem is solved.

What does mankind need to eat in order to live? There are several important elements in our food which we are constantly in danger of forgetting. As a matter of fact, we daily depend upon four most important kinds of food to nourish our life. The first of these is air. In plain talk, we must "eat wind." The second kind of food we need is water. The third is animal food, that is, meat. The fourth is plant food, the five cereals, fruits, and vegetables. Air, water, meat and vegetables are the four vital elements of our food. Air and water are found everywhere. If people live on the banks of streams, they can use running water, otherwise they use water from springs and wells or rain water. Water is to be found everywhere. Air, too, is all around us. So, although air and water are indispensable elements in human subsistence, yet because they are limitless and inexhaustible, because they are bestowed by nature and do not require man's effort, we shall call them "natural gifts." Consequently, they do not constitute problems for us. But animal and plant food are serious problems. Primitive man, like the present-day savages, lived by hunting and fishing; he caught animals in the water and upon land for his food. As civilization advanced, man came to the agricultural stage and learned how to plant the five cereals. He then depended upon plant life for his nourishment. China has had four thousand years of civilization, so we have progressed further in the civilized use of food than Western nations. We depend chiefly upon plants for food. Although plants grow out of the ground, yet much labor must be expended and many various methods must be used before they can be of service to us. If we want to solve the problem of plant food, we must first study the question of production.

Since olden times China has been a farming nation. Agriculture has been the great industry for the production of food. By what methods can we increase plant production? Chinese agriculture has always depended entirely upon human labor, yet cultivation has developed to a very high point and all the various products are of a superior and beautiful quality. Foreign scientists have been led to give high praise to Chinese farming. Since the production of food in China depends upon the peasants, and since the peasants have to toil so bitterly, we must have the government make regulations by law for the protection of peasants if we want to increase the production of food. A large majority of the people in China are peasants, at least nine out of every ten, yet the food which they raise with such wearisome labor is mostly taken away by the landowners. What they themselves can keep is barely sufficient to keep them alive. This is a most unjust situation. If we are to increase the production of food, we must make laws regarding the rights and interests of the farmers; we must give them encouragement and protection and allow them to keep more of the fruit of their land. The protection of the farmers' rights and the giving to them of a larger share in their harvests are questions related to the equalization of land ownership. When the *Min Sheng* Principle is fully realized and the problems of the farmer are all solved, each tiller of the soil will possess his own fields-that is to be the final fruit of our efforts.

What are the real conditions among Chinese farmers? Although China does not have great landowners, yet nine out of ten farmers do not own their fields. Most of the farming land is in the possession of landlords who do not do the cultivating themselves. It seems only right that the farmer should till his farm for himself and claim its products, yet farmers to-day are tilling for others and over half of the agricultural products from the farms are taken by the landlords. We must immediately use gov-ernment and law to remedy this grave situation. Unless we can solve the agrarian problem, there will be no solution for the livelihood problem. Of the food produced in the fields, sixty per cent, according to our latest rural surveys, goes to the landlord, while only forty per cent goes to the farmer. If this unjust state of affairs continues, when the farmers become intelligent, who will still be willing to toil and suffer in the fields? But if the food raised in the fields all goes to the farmers, the farmers will be more eager to farm and production will increase.

In dealing with agricultural production, we should study not only this question of liberating the peasants but also the seven methods of increasing production. These methods are: use of machinery, use of fertilizers, rotation of crops, eradication of pests, manufacturing, transportation, and prevention of natural disasters. The first method is the use of machinery. For these thousands of years China has farmed entirely with man power and has never used machinery. If we should introduce farming machinery, we could at least double China's agricultural production and we could reduce the cost of production to one tenth or one hundredth of what it is now. If China with human labor can support four hundred millions, she should with machine power produce enough for eight hundred millions. If machinery were substituted for human labor in the production of food, then much waste land, which cannot now be cultivated because it is too elevated, might be irrigated with pumps and pipes and opened up to cultivation. Good land already under cultivation could be irrigated by machinery and freed from the danger of drought, thus increasing its productivity. If the old, uncultivated waste land can be opened up, then China naturally will produce more food. The cultivating and pumping machines in use now are all shipped in from other countries, but if the farmers all begin to use machinery and the demand for it increases, then we ought to manufacture our own and recover the profits which are flowing abroad.

The second method of increasing production is the use of fertilizers. In the past China has used night soil and manures, and various kinds of decayed vegetable matter but never chemical fertilizers. Only recently has Chile saltpeter begun to be used for fertilizing in China. Besides Chile saltpeter, the phosphorus from all kinds of Crustacea and the potassium from mineral mountains and cliffs make very good fertilizers. If compounds of nitrogen, phosphorus, and potassium are combined, an excellent fertilizer is formed, which makes the cultivation of any plant easy and greatly stimulates production. For example, an unfertilized *mow* of land will produce five baskets of corn, but if the same *mow* be fertilized, the crop will be two or three times as large. So to increase production we must apply fertilizers to the land, and in order to apply fertilizers we must study science and manufacture fertilizers by scientific methods. China has the raw materials for fertilizers everywhere. The material in Chile saltpeter was long ago used by the Chinese in the manufacture of gunpowder. Formerly all fertilizers which the world used were produced in Chile, but with the advance of science, scientists have discovered a new method of manufacturing nitrates by use of electricity. So now the different countries do not have to depend upon natural sodium nitrate shipped from Chile, but are manufacturing artificial nitrates by means of electricity. The artificial nitrates are just as effective as natural nitrates and require very little initial expenditure; consequently people in every country gladly use them.

How is electricity generated? The ordinary, expensive electricity is generated by steam power but the newer and cheaper kind of electricity is all generated by water power. Recently foreign countries have begun to use their waterfalls and rapids for driving their dynamos. Enormous electric power can be generated in this way, and the power can be used manufacture artifical nitrates. The natural power of waterfalls and rapids does not cost anything and consequently the price of the electricity generated is very low. With cheap electric power, the manufactured, artificial nitrates are inexpensive.

If we could make use of the Yangtze and the Yellow River water power to generate a hundred million horse power, or twenty-four hundred million man power, and let this great electrical energy work for us, China would produce a great deal, and would certainly turn her poverty into riches. So in the matter of agricultural production, if we can improve upon human labor and use machinery, if, moreover, we can use electric power to manufacture fertillzers, we can certainly greatly increase the yield of our fields.

The third method of increasing production is crop rotation. This means planting different thing or different brands of seed on the same piece of land in successive years. For example, Kwangtung seed might be planted this year; Hunan seed, next year; and Szechuan seed, year after next. What advantage is there in such rotation? It means change and rest for the various soils and increase in crop yield. When the seeds fall into new soil and spring up in fresh atmosphere, the plants are stronger and the harvest is more abundant. Thus crop rotation increases production.

The fouth method is eradication of pests. On the farm there are both plants and animals which are injurious. For example, rice is to be planted in the fields, but at the time of planting all sorts of malformed grain stalks and weeds spring up very fast and hinder the growth of the rice as well as suck the fertility of the soil. They are very harmful to the rice. The farmer should use scientific principles and study how to get rid of these noxious darnel and weeds and so prevent their injuring the crop; at the same time he should find out if there is any way to use them to increase the yield. What animals are pests? There are numerous species. One of the most common is the locust. If the locust or any other of the injurious insects attacks a ripening plant, it gnaws and destroys the plant so that there is no crop. There are many other kinds of injurious insects, and the state should employ specialists to make a careful study of them and to find ways to eradicate them. The United States now is much concerned over these problems and is spending a great deal of money every year in a study of methods for destroying pests. Consequently, the income from agriculture is showing an annual increase of hundreds of millions. We must use the great power of the state and imitate the United States' methods of destroying injurious insects, then agricultural pests throughout the country will diminish and production will increase.

The fifth method of increasing production is by manufacture. If food is to be preserved for a long time and to be sent to distant places, it must pass through a preserving process. In out country the most common methods of preserving foods are by drying and salting: we have dried vegetables, dried fish, dried meat, salted vegetables, salted fish, salted meat, and so on. Recently a new method has been introduced in the West: the food is first thoroughly cooked by boiling or baking, then put into cans and the cans sealed. No matter how long the food is kept, it has a fresh flavor when taken from the cans. This is the best method of preserving food; any kind of fish, meat, fruit, vegetable, or biscuit can be canned and distributed throughout the country or sold abroad.

The sixth method of increasing production is by means of transportation. When there is a surplus of food, we must begin to exchange; we must take the surplus here and make it supply the deficiency there. For example, the Three Eastern Provinces of Manchuria* and North China have beans and wheat but no rice, while all the southern provinces have rice but little beans and wheat. We ought to take the surplus beans and wheat from Manchuria and North China and send them to South China and use the surplus rice in south China to supply North China and Manchuria. But such an ex-

* Later, Manchuria was divided into nine provinces.

change of good depends upon means of transportation. The greatest problem now in China is that of transportation. A great deal of waste results from unsuitable methods. Because of our imperfect means of transportation in the past, the most valuable and necessary food has not been able to circulate freely, and the food problem has remained unsolved.

China's best means of transportation have been natural waterways and canals. The Grand Canal is a very long stream; it commences at Hangchow, passes through Soochow, Chinkiang, Yangchow, Shantung, and Tientsin and comes to an end finally at Tungchow, not far from Peiping after tranversing a total distance of three thousand *li.* It is indeed the world's longest canael. Such a waterway is extremely convenient, and if the number of modern steamboats and motor boats upon it were increased, it would be yet more serviceable. Little attention, however, has been paid of late to the Grand Canal. If we want to solve the food problem of the future and be able to transport food easily, we must restore the old canal system. The present Grand Canal should be repaired and the canal system should be extended to where no waterways at present exist. In transportation upon the sea we need large steamships, for the world's most inexpensive way of carrying freight is by water.

Next in cheapness comes railway transportation. If railroads could be built in the eighteen provinces of China, in Sinkiang, Manchuria, Chinghai (Kokonor), Tibet, Inner and Outer Mongolia, and all these railroads could be linked together in one system, China's food supply could circulate in all directions, and people in every part of the country would have cheap food to eat. So railways are one good means of solving the food problem. Railroads, however, can be built only through busy and prosperous sections of the country where they can make money. If they are built through poor country and obscure sections, there will not be much produce to transport nor many passengers to carry. The railways would not only make no profits but would lose money. So we cannot construct railroads through poor and remote country; in such sections we should build only motor roads upon which motor cars can travel. The large cities would then have railroads and the small towns and villages motor roads and all these roads could be connected in a complete system of transportation. The large cities could use the big trains and the small towns and villages motor cars for food transportation. When the motor road is built, only the poor and remote communities which the road does not traverse will have to use coolie transportation. From this we see that four means are essential if we are to solve the question of food transportation: first, canals; second, railroads; third, motor roads; and fourth, coolie transportation. If we develop these four means of transportation in the best way, our four hundred millions will have cheap food to eat.

The seventh method of increasing agricultural production is prevention of natural disasters. How shall we go about preventing a flood? Last year I saw some high dikes along the Tung Kiang. They are all strongly built and can help to prevent flood disaster yet not be broken down by the rush of the waters. This dike-building method is regulative and puts a check upon the waters. But it is only half of the method for flood prevention and cannot entirely control the waters. Besides building dikes, we must also deepen the rivers and harbors and dredge all the silt and sand along the bottoms. If there is no silt in the harbors to hinder the flow of rivers and the river beds are deep, then it will be easy for the waters to pass out to set, the rivers will not overflow everywhere, and flood calamities will be reduced. So the deepening of waterways and the building of high dikes are two kinds of engineering which must be carried out simultaneously if we want to keep the rivers in complete control.

But what about fundamental methods of flood prevention? Why is it that flood disasters are becoming more common every year now? Why were floods very rare in olden times? Because in the old days there were extensive forests; but too much timber has been cut off by the people and the land has not been reforested. As a result there are now very few forests, while numerous mountains and ranges are completely bare. When a heavy rain falls, the mountain sides have no forests to absorb the rain or to check the flow of rain water, and so the water off the mountains flows immediately into the rivers, the rivers immediately swell, and a devastating flood follows. Hence, forestation has an important bearing upon the prevention of floods. The planting of more forests is the fundamental method of flood prevention. Then, when the heavy rains come, the branches and leaves of the trees will absorb the water in the air, and the roots will absorb the water on the ground. Very thick forest can absorb a tremendous amount of water. The water thus collected by the trees flows gradually down to the rivers, rather than directly and suddenly, and does not cause floods. The radical method of flood prevention, then, is forestation. So if, in order to solve the food problem, we want to prevent floods, we must first create forests. Then we can avert flood evil throughout the country. Reforestation of the whole country, in the final analysis, must be carried out bv the state. Only under direction can such an enterprise easily succeed.

Then there are also drought disasters. How are we to deal with the problem of drought? People used to think that droughts were fixed by fate and could not be prevented. But as science advances, ways are being found to avert all kinds of natural disasters. The prevention of droughts requires also the strength of the whole nation and a broad, unified plan. The fundamental method in this plan is, again, forestation. Where forests grow, there is a more suitable proportion of moisture in the air, rains are frequent, and droughts are much less common. For high land and places without springs, we can arrange to pump water by machinery, thus relieving their drought. This irrigation method of preventing droughts may be compared to the dike method of preventing floods—both are only regulative. The regulative methods make it possible to save the situation when floods or droughts come suddenly. The radical method of preventing floods or droughts is forestation—forestation on a national scale. The regulative methods depend upon the use of pumping machinery, upon the building of high dikes, and the deepening of waterways. If we can fully carry out both the regulative and the radical measures, we can avert flood and drought, and then the food produce of our land will not be lost.

If China can liberate the farmers and put into effect the seven methods of increasing agricultural production which I have described, will our food problem then be completely solved? Even if we succeed beautifully in dealing with these questions of production, we will not have completely solved our food problem. You all know that the European and American nations have all been founded upon industry commerce, but you may not know that their industrialized and commercialized governments devote a great deal of time also to the study of agricultural problems. The United States, for example, omits nothing of the smallest significance in the study of rural problems for the improvement of rural life. The government not only makes detailed investigations of agricultural conditions in the home country, but constantly sends specialists to the interior of China, to Manchuria, Mongolia , and other places, in order to learn about conditions there. They take Chinese methods of farming and all kinds of Chinese seeds back to the United States to test and to use. The United States of late has been placing great emphasis upon agriculture; railway facilities for transporting food, means of preventing natural disasters, and all kinds of scientific equipment are complete and up to date.

Yet has the United States really solved her food problem? I do not think that she has. Every year the United States ships vast quantities of food for sale in other countries and her food supply is abundant—why, then, do I say that her food problem is unsolved? Because agriculture in the United States is still controlled by capitalists. Under the system of private capital which still exists, methods of production are over developed, while on attention at all is paid to proper methods of distribution. So the problem of livelihood cannot be solved. In order to reach a solution, we must not only deal with questions of production but must also lay emphasis upon the questions of distribution. Equitable methods of distribution are impossible under a system of private capital, for under such a system all production heads towards one goal—profit. Since the production of food aims at profit, when food prices are low in the native country, the food will be shipped for sale and greater profits abroad. Just because private individuals want to make more money! Even when there is a native famine, when the people are short of food and many are starving, these private capitalists are not concerned. With such methods of distribution, which aim wholly at profit, the problem of livelihood can never be well solved. If we want to carry out the *Min Sheng* Principle we must give thought to methods of distribution—methods which will aim not at profit, but at supplying the people with food. Our *Min Sheng* Principle aims at the destruction of the capitalistic system. China already has an inadequate food supply, yet every year we still ship a lot of food to other countries to be sold because a group of capitalists want to make money.

If we apply the *Min Sheng* Principle we must make the aim of food production not profit but the provision of sustenance for all the people. To do this we must store up the surplus in production every year. Not only must we wait to see if this year's food supply is sufficient, we must wait until the supply next year and the year after is abundant before we ship any food for sale abroad. If after three years the food supply is still short, we will not make any shipments abroad. If we can apply the *Min Sheng* Principle in this way and make the support of the people rather than profit the aim of production, then there will be hope for an abundant food supply in China. The fundamental difference, then, between the Principle of Livelihood and capitalism is this: capitalism makes profit its sole aim, while the Principle of Livelihood makes the nurture of the people its aim. With such a noble principle we can destroy the old, evil capitalistic system.

But in applying the *Min Sheng* Principle for the solution of China's food problems, we can only make gradual changes in the capitalistic system; we must not try to overthrow it immediately. Our first aim is to give China an abundant food supply; when this is realized, it will be easy to go the next step and greatly reduce the price of food.

What shall be our plan for the distribution

of food? Food is the greatest need of the people as they seek for their livelihood. Economist have always spoken of three necessities of life—food, clothing, and shelter. My study leads me to add a fourth necessity, an extremely important one—means of travel. In order to solve the livelihood problem we must not only greatly reduce the cost of these four necessities, but we must make them available for all the people of the nation. If the *San Min* Principles are to become effective and a new world is to be built up, then no one must lack any of these four necessities of life. It is essential that the state undertake the responsibility for providing these necessities; anyone should be able to call the state to task if it does not provide enough of each. The state must shoulder the burden of meeting the people's living needs. What of the people's responsibility to the state? The people have very definite obligations: the farmer must produce food, the industrial worker must manufacture tools, the business man must connect supply and demand, the scholar must devote his intelligence and ability—every man must fulfill his duty. Then all will be supplied with the four necessities of life.

We are studying the *Min Sheng* Principle in order to solve the problems involved in these four necessities. Today I have begun by discussing the food problem. The first step in dealing with the food problem is to solve the problem of production; then comes the problem of distribution. In order to have a fair and equitable distribution of food, we must save food every year. Only when we have saved enough for three years' food supply will we ship any surplus for sale abroad. Such a plan of saving grain is like the old system of public granaries.* In recent times, however, the public granary system has broken down, and this, together with foreign economic domination, has resulted in widespread poverty and national bankruptcy. So now is the criti-

* The public granaries distributed grain to the poor in time of need.

cal time to solve our livelihood problem. If we fail to take advantage of the present time and wait till some future day, we will find the task harder than ever. Our Kuomintang sets forth the Three Principles of the People as the basis upon which to build our new nation. As we work out the Principle of Livelihood, let us not merely emphasize the theories connected with it, let us also pay serious attention to its practical application.

LECTURE FOUR

Delivered on August 24, 1924.

The subject of my lecture to-day is the problem of clothing. The first important problem in the Principle of Livelihood is food, the next problem is clothing, and that is what I shall discuss now. Only man, only civilized man in fact, wears clothing. Other animals and the plants do not have clothes to wear, nor do savages wear clothes. Food, then, is the chief problem of livelihood and clothing is the second. The uncivilized races of Africa and Malaysia go without clothes, and so our primitive ancestors must also have lived naked. The wearing of clothes has come with the progress of civilization; the more civilization advances, the more complex becomes the problem of clothing. The more civilization advanced, the more complete clothing became.

How far have we got towards a solution of the clothing problem? Clothing is one of the necessities of life. In the progress of human civilization, living standards evolve through three stages. The first stage is that of necessities. Without these necessities human life of course cannot exist, and without a sufficient amount of them, life is incomplete, half dead and half alive. The necessities of the first stage man could not do without. Then man advanced to the second stage, the stage of comforts. When man reached this standard of living, he began to seek not only the necessary things of life but also joy and comfort. Then he went a step further and looked for luxuries. Take clothing, for example. In ancient times "grass cloth in summer and fur in winter" were considered ample. But when man reached the standard of comfort, he was not content with clothing that should simply meet his physical needs; he wanted his clothing also to fit his body and to be comfortable. Later man advanced another step and began to seek beauty and refinement in his clothing—light raw silks and delicate lustering in place of grass cloth in the summer; otter and sable furs in place of ordinary animal furs in the winter. Thus the wearing of clothing has developed from the wearing of plain, necessary clothing to the wearing of comfortable clothing, and from the wearing of comfortable clothing to the wearing of beautiful and luxurious clothing. In the same way the eating of food has evolved. At first man simply sought to fill his stomach with "green vegetables and coarse rice." Then he began to desire the sweet and juicy flavors of wine and cooked meat. Further on, he began to comb the mountains and the seas for delicacies and dainties.

But in seeking a solution for the problem of livelihood we are not dealing with comforts or with luxuries; we are simply trying to solve the problem of necessities. We want the four hundred millions throughout the nation to have the necessary food and clothing, enough to eat and to wear. The first step towards a solution of the problem is a study of how materials for clothing are produced. Clothing materials come from animals and plants—two kinds from animals and two kinds from plants. These four materials are silk, hemp or flax, cotton, and wool. Cotton and hemp are secured from plants, silk and wool from animals. Silk is spun by the *Ch'an* or silk-worm; wool grows upon the backs of camels and other animals. These four products are the essential materials for man's clothing.

Let us first consider silk. Silk is a fine material for clothes and was first discovered in China. The Chinese in very ancient times wore silks. Although the civilization of the Western Powers has now far outstripped ours, yet at the time when China discovered silk, their peoples were still in the age of savagery and were still "eating raw meat and drinking blood." Not until two or three centuries ago did their civilization begin to advance beyond ours and did they learn to use silk as the material for beautiful clothes. Now Westerners use silk to make some necessities but chiefly to make articles of luxury.

Although China discovered silk several thousand years ago, yet the key to the clothing problem of our four hundred millions is not silk. Our necessary articles of clothing are not made of silk, and a large proportion of the people cannot afford to wear silk.

Our silk industry, the methods of producing silk and of making silk goods which we discovered, was once all very fine. But we did not know how to make improvements; and later when foreigners copied our industry, applied modern science to it and introduced improvements in it, they were able to make silk superior to Chinese silk and to supplant the Chinese silk industry. Investigation will show that the decline of the Chinese silk industry is due to poor methods of production. A great many Chinese silkworms are diseased; in fact, half the silkworms in every crop turn out badly and die before maturity. If by chance they live, the raw silk from the cocoons of diseased silkworms does not make goods of fine quality or color. Our methods of silk reeling are also imperfect; the threads have too many breaks in them and not suited to the use of foreign silk looms. Consequently, Chinese silk has gradually lost out in competition with foreign silk. Several decades ago the foreign methods of sericulture were just like the Chinese methods. When the Chinese farmer raises silkworms, the results are sometimes good; at other times, there is a complete loss of the crop. The farmer has no other way to explain such different outcomes but to attribute them to fate. This was also the case with foreign farmers. Then scientists began to discover the principles of biology and to study minutely all forms of life, not only those visible to the naked eye, but also, by means of microscopes which magnified thousands of times, those too small for the naked eye.

In the course of such investigations, a French scientist named Pasteur made the discovery that all diseases of animals, whether of human beings or of silkworms, are caused by minute organisms, or microbes. Unless these microbes can be destroyed, the diseased animal will surely die. After spending much time and making extended researches, Pasteur understood thoroughly the nature of these micro-organisms and was able to discover methods to eradicate them and so to rid the silkworms of disease. When these methods were communicated to the silk growers of France and Italy, the diseased silkworms were greatly reduced in number and the cocoon spinning turned out very well. The silk industry was then able to make great progress. Later on, Japan began to study these methods and her silk industry began to advance. China's farmers, however, have always been conservative and unwilling to learn new methods, so our silk industry has steadily declined.

If China is to reform her silk industry and to increase silk production, her silk growers must learn foreign scientific methods and must improve the silkworm egg and mulberry leaves; they must also study the best methods of reeling the silk from the cocoons and of sorting and improving the various grades, qualities, and colors of raw silk. Then China's silk industry will gradually progress and will be able to compete in the world's silk market. If Chinese do not improve their mulberry leaves and silkworm eggs and the quality of the raw silk, but stick to the old methods, China's silk industry will not only fail but will probably, in the course of natural selection, be utterly wiped out. Most of the people now in China do not wear silk, but our raw silk is shipped abroad in exchange for cotton fabrics and yarn. If Chinese silk is poor in quality, other countries will not want it and the silk will have no market. China then will not only lose one of her chief sources of wealth, but she will also have no material for making clothing, since she cannot export her silk in exchange for cotton goods and yarn. So if China wants her people to have the material necessary for clothing in order to solve their clothing problem, she must preserve her ancient industry, improve her silkworm eggs and mulberry leaves and reform her methods of silk reeling. China's gauzes and satins used to be very fine, unexcelled in any foreign country. But now the silk goods which come from foreign machine looms are much superior to Chinese goods. The exquisite silk goods which are now being used by wealthy Chinese families all come from abroad, which shows how our splendid native industry has been ruined. To solve the silk problem, we must not only improve silkworm eggs and mulberry leaves, and reform methods of sericulture and of silk reeling in order to produce better silk, but we must also learn foreign methods of weaving silks and satins by machinery. Then we can make beautiful silk goods for the use of our people; when the home demand is met, we can ship the surplus abroad in exchange for other goods.

The second material of which clothes are

made is hemp. Hemp also owes its first discovery to China. In ancient times the Chinese found the method for making cloth from hemp, and this old method is still followed by all today. But Chinese agriculture never progresses, so the linen industry has recently been taken from us by other countries. All the provinces China raise hemp to a great extent, but the goods made from hemp are suitable only for summer clothing and do not last more than one season. If we want better the linen industry, we must make a detailed and radical study of its agricultural side—how to cultivate hemp and flax and how to apply fertilizers; and also of its manufacturing side—how to produce fine linen thread. Then linen industry will develop and manufactured linen goods will be inexpensive. In the past the linen industry has depended solely upon hand labor; no machinery has been used. Hand manufacture not only consumes time and produces poor linen fabrics but also requires expsensive capital. If we want to improve the linen industry and manufacture linen fabrics, we must have a broad plan. All along the line, from the fields, where the hemp or flax is grown, to the factories, where linen fabrics are woven, we must apply the most modern scientific methods. If we can effect such a reform, then we shall get good linens and inexpensive material for clothing.

Silk and hemp as raw material for clothing were first discovered in China. But clothes nowadays are made not only of silk and hemp or flax; most clothes are made of cotton, while wool is being used to an increasing extent. Cotton and wool are now necessary material for everyone's clothing. Cotton is not native to China; the Ceiba tree cotton* was introduced from India. After China obtained cotton seeds from India and began to plant them in various sections of the country, and after she learned how to spin and to weave cotton, a cotton industry was built up. Lately,

* Referring to what is commercially known as "Indian cottons"

however, foreign cotton cloth of a better quality than the native cloth, and quite inexpensive, has been imported into China. Chinese have preferred the foreign to the native cloth, and so our native industry has been driven to the wall. This means that Chinese have to depend upon foreign countries for the necessary clothing material. Small native industries still in existence use foreign yarn in the weaving. You can see from this how the bottom has been knocked out of our cloth industry by other countries.

Although China produces a great deal of cotton of good natural quality, yet, because her industries are undeveloped, she cannot herself use the raw cotton in the manufacture of good fabrics and yarn; she can only ship it for sale abroad. The clothes we wear every day are made of imported material for which we have to pay a high price. The high price we pay is the sending of our valuable money and food abroad in settlement. Such is the present condition of China under foreign economic domination.

Foreign nations do not oppress China with economic power alone. When foreign nations at times find their economic strength weak and cannot attain their objectives in other ways, they add political force. In former days China's handwork competed against foreign machinery and lost out, but that was purely an economic problem. The failure after the European War of Chinese spinning and textile factories, which were competing against foreign nations with machinery modeled after theirs, was not an economic but a political problem. What methods do foreign nations use· in their political domination over China? After the Manchu Government had carried on wars with foreign nations and had been defeated, China was forced to sign many unequal treaties. Foreign nations are still using these treaties to bind China, and as a result China fails at whatever she attempts. If China stood on an equal political basis with other nations, she could compete freely with them in the economic field and be able to hold her own without failure. But as soon as foreign nations use political power as a shield for their economic designs, then China is at a loss how to resist or to compete successfully with them.

If we want to solve our livelihood problem and protect our native industries so that they cannot be attacked by foreign industries, we must first have the political power to protect them. But China to-day in the grip of the treaties has not only lost her sovereign rights and the power to protect her own industries, but is actually giving protection to foreign industries. This comes of the capitalistic expansion, mechanical progress, and economic superiority of foreign countries; besides, foreign economic power is backed up by political power.

In order to compete with other countries we must imitate the tariff policy of the Western nations. What has been their experience with this policy? Several decades ago, British industries ranked first in the world; whatever goods the world needed were all supplied by Great Britain. The United States at that time was still in the agricultural stage; the small industries which existed were being crushed by British industries and had no chance to develop. Then the United States adopted a protective policy and put a protective tariff into effect. All British goods imported into the United States had to pay a heavy duty of fifty to one hundred per cent *ad valorem.* This made the wholesale price of British goods so high that they were unable to compete with American goods. Many kinds of British goods could no longer be shipped to the United States, and American industries began to grow until now they surpass British industries. Several decades ago Germany was also an agricultural nation and the German people also had to depend upon Great Britain for the goods which they needed. They were under the domination of British industry. Later, when Germany adopted a protective policy, her industries also began to develop. In recent years German industries have gone ahead of every other nation's.

It is clear from this that if we want Chinese industries to flourish, we must follow the protective policy of the United States and of Germany, resist the invasion of foreign goods, and protect our native goods. We cannot find a solution for the livelihood problem in the economic field alone; we must take hold on the political side, abolish all unequal treaties, and take back the customs out of foreign control. Then we can freely increase the tariff and put into effect a protective policy. Such a policy will prevent foreign goods from pouring into China, and our home industries will naturally be able to develop.

The most important raw materials which must consider in dealing with our clothing problem are silk, hemp, cotton, and wool. The fourth material, wool, is produced in considerable quantity in China. Chinese wool is superior in quality to foreign wool, but the woolen industry is not developed in China; we do not manufacture woolens but ship our wool to other countries to be sold. Other countries take our wool, make it into woolen goods, and send these back for sale and profit making in China. If we could recover our rights and employ the power of the state to develop our woolen industry, it would flourish along with the cotton industry. If we had a prosperous woolen industry, then Chinese would not have to buy the woolen goods which they need in winter from foreign countries. If we have a surplus of wool which we can market it abroad in the same way as we do our silk. But now the woolen industry is undeveloped in China, so the pelts and the loose cut wool which cannot be used in China are sold at a low price abroad, made into woolen cloth and all kinds of felt goods, shipped back to China, and sold for our money here. This shows that both our cotton and woolen industries are suffering from foreign political and economic domination. In order to solve the clothing problem, we must utilize the great strength of the entire nation in a broad comprehensive plan, first recover our sovereign rights, employ the state's power to develop the agricultural and manufacturing industries in connection with silk, hemp, cotton, and wool, and take back our Maritime Customs for the protection of these industries, raising the duties upon exported raw materials and upon imported manufactured goods. Then our spinning and textile industries will immediately begin to grow and the problem of clothing will reach a solution.

Now that we see the solution for the problem of clothing materials, let us turn to the matter of clothing itself. The wearing of clothes began, I said once before, as a protection against cold. The first function of clothing, then, was protection of the body. But as civilization advanced, clothes began to be used as bodily ornament and the second function of clothing came to be beautification, "presenting a fine appearance." Savage man did not have any clothing for ornament, so he tattooed his body; that is, he marked and colored his flesh, Our ancients called this *wenshen,* or decorating the body. Although civilization has advanced, yet bodily ornament is still considered the chief function of clothing, and the functions of defense against cold and bodily protection are almost forgotten. In this day of high living and extra vagant competition, not only are clothing materials constantly appearing in new forms, but the styles of clothes every year show differences in size and changes in the tastes dictated by custom. More and more are clothes and ornaments considered a mark of worth, and the existence of gentry and *literati* considered as synonymous with cultural progress.

When autocracy developed, clothing was used to distinguish ranks. The third function of clothing was then to mark class distinctions. Now democracy prevails and our classes are levelled down. However, the file and rank of the army and navy in a Republic are still identified by their uniform. To the three functions of clothing just mentioned–physical protection, bodily ornament, and class distinction–we must add a fourth, convenience. For we are considering clothing as the people's necessity in a day when all classes are becoming equal and labor is becoming sacred. Let us say, then, that the clothing needed by our people must fulfill all following functions–it must protect the body, it must be good-looking, and it must be convenient and not hinder work. Such clothing will truly be fine.

In order to carry out the Principle of Livelihood and with these three uses of clothing in mind, the state should establish clothing factories everywhere on a large scale. These factories should manufacture the clothing needed by the people, according to the population and temperature of the seasons in the various sections of the country. Everyone should be supplied with the necessary clothing; not one person should be left out. This is the duty which the government of the *San Min Chu I* state owes to its people with respect to the necessity of clothing.

And the people must of course fulfill the obligations of citizenship to the state or disqualify themselves as citizens. Those who disqualify themselves as citizens disqualify themselves as masters of the state. Lazy vagabonds are parasites upon the state and upon the people. The government should force them by law to work and try to convert them into honorable laborers, worthy to share in the rights and privileges of the nation. When loafers are eliminated and all men have a share in production, then there will be enough to eat and to wear, homes will be comfortable, and the people will be content, and the problem of livelihood will be solved.*

* The lectures upon the Principle of Livelihood were never completed by Dr. Sun.

書　　名：**三民主義**

SAN MIN CHU I

(THE THREE PRINCIPLES OF PEOPLE)

作　　者：孫中山先生

Dr. SUN YAT-SEN

印 行 者：美加各界推廣三民主義募印委員會

SAN MIN CHU I SOCIETY

美國地址：836 STOCKTON ST.

SAN FRANCISCO, CA 94108 USA

TEL:(415)982-6218　FAX:(415)982-3025

加拿大地址：529 GORE AVE,

VANCOUVER, B.C. CANADA V6A 2Z6

TEL:(604)681-6022　FAX:(604)682-6624

出版日期：2003 年（民國 92 年）十月初版

初版印數：中文本壹萬冊，英文本五千冊，光碟壹萬五千片

承 印 者：海宇文化事業有限公司

台北市中華路一段 104 號

HAI YU COLTURAL IND,

104, 1 SEC. CHUNG HWA ROAD

TAIPEI, TAIWAN, R.O.C.

TEL:(02)2331-3056　FAX:(02)2331-9097

定　　價：中文本或英文本，每本美金 5 元（郵費另計）

US$5.00　PER COPY